The New
Dynamics
of Winning

John Mazzec

Also by Denis Waitley

Books

The Psychology of Winning
The Winner's Edge
Seeds of Greatness
The Joy of Working
Timing Is Everything

Audiotapes

The Psychology of Winning
Seeds of Greatness
Quantum Breakthrough to Excellence
(with Irving Dardik)
Denis Waitley Live
The Double Win
The Inner Winner
The Joy of Working
(with Reni Witt)
The Subliminal Winner
(with Dr. Thomas Budzynski)
Being the Best
Breakthrough Thinking
(with Robert Tucker)
How to Build Your Child's Self-Esteem
The Course in Winning
The Optimal You (with Dr. Thomas Budzynski)
The New Dynamics of Winning
The Psychology of Human Motivation

The New Dynamics of Winning

Gain the Mind-set of a Champion

for Unlimited Success in

Business and Life

Denis Waitley

William Morrow and Company, Inc.

New York

It is the policy of William Morrow and Company, Inc., and its imprints and affiliates, recognizing the importance of preserving what has been written, to print the books we publish on acid-free paper, and we exert our best efforts to that end.

Library of Congress Cataloging-in-Publication Data

Waitley, Denis.
    The new dynamics of winning / by Denis Waitley.
        p.   cm.
    Includes bibliographical references.
    ISBN 0-688-11562-4
    1. Success—Psychological aspects.   2. Sports—Psychological
aspects.   I. Title.
BF637.S8W268   1993
158′.2—dc20

92-20907
CIP

Printed in the United States of America

First Edition

1   2   3   4   5   6   7   8   9   10

BOOK DESIGN BY BARBARA COHEN ARONICA

To the real champions in life,
those unsung heroes and heroines,
the role models, mentors, and coaches
who teach us how to win,
watching quietly from the sidelines,
with inner pride,
as we act out their knowledge and experience
and claim the medals and the fame
as our own.

ACKNOWLEDGMENTS

Thanks to Vic Conant and his management team at Nightingale-Conant Corporation, who brought me from the grandstand into the arena.

And to Jill Schacter, my executive editor at Nightingale-Conant, whose special talents, insights, and patience have challenged me to greater heights.

To Mitch Sisskind, whose writing ability and creativity should win a gold medal for converting the spoken word into a worthy manuscript.

And to the William Morrow publishing staff, truly unbeatable in every respect!

CONTENTS

INTRODUCTION

What does it take to be a winner? What *must you know* to be a true champion—in athletics, in business, and in life?

I've devoted my career to studying peak performers in every field, and the single most important fact I've learned is this: *Being a champion means thinking like a champion.* With *The New Dynamics of Winning,* that's exactly what you'll learn to do.

As an achievement-oriented person, you've probably asked yourself how you should go about attaining your goals. Perhaps the answers you've come up with have worked well for you. Perhaps you're still looking for the answers. But there's one thing of which I'm absolutely certain: You *already have* the talent, the intelligence, and more than enough of any other necessary resource to achieve virtually anything you could possibly want, in both your career and your personal life.

Unfortunately, that's not enough.

Because you've got to know how to put those resources to work. You've got to be able to transform ability into tangible accomplishments. And that's where this book can help.

In the intensely competitive world of international athletics, the Russians and the East Germans were the first to understand the all-important psychological component of winning. As head of the mental training program for the United States Olympic Committee's Sports Medicine Council during the early 1980s, I was able to adapt many of their methods for use by American athletes, and also to follow the development of additional breakthrough techniques.

With *The New Dynamics of Winning,* you'll have the benefit of everything I learned in my work with the Olympians—as well as with Super Bowl champions, astronauts, Fortune 500 executives, and successful entrepreneurs. Remember: You already have the potential to live your dreams. By the time you finish this book, you'll have the practical mental skills to achieve peak performance in any setting you choose.

Some of the major points we'll cover include:

- The most important traits of a champion
- The five most prevalent self-destructive beliefs
- How to focus your mind for peak performance, anywhere, anytime
- The important relationship between integrity and success
- The secrets of mental toughness, and how to overcome setbacks
- The components of effective leadership and the importance of coachability
- How "paying the price" prepares you for success
- How to use stress to your advantage

It took years of hard work by many talented people—and it cost many thousands of dollars—to gain the theoretical understanding and the practical applications that make up this book. These are the principles that helped Bill Toomey win the Olympic gold medal in the decathlon, and that powered Greg LeMond to victory in the Tour de France.

They're the same principles that have helped build the careers of some of the wealthiest, most successful men and women in America.

They are *The New Dynamics of Winning.* I urge you to put them to work for you.

—Denis Waitley

The New
Dynamics
of Winning

The Drive to Win

The Mind-set of a Champion

The human spirit . . . the triumph over pain . . . the new dynamics of winning. On July 23, 1989, they all come together in one unforgettable moment.

A young man on a bicycle is speeding along the roads of France. His mind is focused on just one thing—get to Paris as fast as he possibly can. His name is Greg LeMond. And in the final leg of the Tour de France, the world's most famous bike race, Greg LeMond, from Wayzata, Minnesota, is performing one of the most remarkable feats in the history of any sport.

For a moment, pretend you're there with him. Try to imagine what he feels: pain, fatigue, perhaps doubt that the task can be successfully accomplished, but at the same time, an unshakable determination to give the very best effort possible. I want you, through your imagination, to put yourself as close as you can to Greg LeMond in that race.

It's vitally important that you do this. Because you, and all of us in American business, are facing a situation that's very much analogous to that which confronted Greg LeMond in 1989. It makes no difference whether you're part of a large corporation, or own a business, or make your living in sales and marketing.

You want to build a good life for yourself and your family. You're determined to provide for the education of your children, and for your own retirement, and for all the things you want to do *right now*. But you're living in a global village where competition, change, and complexity are increasing at unprecedented speed. The unexpected is occurring on a daily basis. The opportunities are still there, certainly, but you're going to have to prepare yourself differently, train more thoroughly, act more intelligently and proactively and anticipate future trends. You're going to have to make them happen.

What will it take to succeed? Hard work, of course. Careful decision-making. Technical expertise. The support of friends and family. Those are all part of it, but what's *most important* is your ability to access the inner resources of strength and commitment that are the defining characteristics of a champion in any field.

In these pages, I'll help you to do that. I'll show you how the same mental training and self-motivating techniques that worked for champions like Greg LeMond can work for you.

- You'll benefit from psychological research that has uncovered the keys to peak performance, so that you, too, can develop the mental traits of a winner.

- You'll discover the inner skills and motivating habits of elite athletes, and you'll learn to apply them in your own working life.

- You'll gain the ability to block out distractions and negative influences, in order to achieve total concentration.

- You'll be able to make stress and pressure work for you instead of against you in any situation, no matter how intense.

Now, picture this: LeMond starts fifty seconds behind the leader, Laurent Fignon of France. The final leg of the race is just twenty-four kilometers, or about fifteen miles—too short a distance for LeMond to have a chance of catching Fignon.

The French are already celebrating. Fignon is a certain winner. That's what the experts say.

But the experts can't see into the mind and heart of Greg LeMond. The experts can't see his burning desire or his willingness to pay the price for victory. The experts write off Greg LeMond, but the man himself never gives up. Because he's already overcome something bigger than just fifty seconds in a bike race—he's had to fight the greatest battle of all: the fight to stay alive.

Greg LeMond is racing toward Paris with thirty shotgun pellets in his body. Two of them are in his heart.

In April, 1987, on a hunting trip at a ranch near Lincoln, California, LeMond, his uncle, and brother-in-law split up while in the woods. Because they couldn't see each other, a disaster occurred. A shotgun blast broke the silence, and sixty number-two-size shotgun pellets ripped through the back and side of Greg LeMond. His brother-in-law had accidentally shot him.

Greg thought he was dying, but a helicopter rescued him. He was taken to a hospital and somehow he survived. He endured the worst pain he had ever known, but he made it. Somehow champions always do. It's 10 percent talent and 90 percent guts and determination. All this made Greg LeMond a superstar. He'd already won the Tour de France in 1986, the first person from outside Europe ever to win this great race. After the accident, all his inner qualities, all that mental fortitude, brought him back from the edge of death.

Not only did he recover, but he returned to bike racing, even though thirty of those shotgun pellets were still inside his body. The road back to a championship was brutal and punishing. It was so hard that at one point he almost quit.

The same year as the accident he went back into ~~the hos~~pital for another operation, this time for appendicitis. After being almost completely out of action for twelve months, he suffered a tendon injury the following year that required surgery, and he had to give up nearly another full summer of racing. But champions are made of special stuff, and Greg LeMond hung in.

And it all pays off on that warm day in July.

Suddenly, LeMond is going faster and faster. No one can believe what's happening. You can't gain ground that fast. But he's doing it. His concentration is all-consuming. He's not watching his own time, he's not watching Fignon's time. Instead, he's totally focused on what he's doing, *willing* his way to victory.

Now he's in Paris. He passes the Champs-Élysées, then the Arc de Triomphe . . .

He's pumping, fighting for every second he can get. He streaks across the finish line . . .

And Greg LeMond wins the Tour de France by scarcely the length of a bicycle.

The Zone, and How to Get There

Greg LeMond's win was a triumph of spirit and hope. A win over pain, frustration, and the odds. It's a victory we can all admire. More than that, it's an accomplishment you and I can learn from and use in every area of our lives.

What's the secret? It's being able to put yourself into the state of mind that Greg achieved during the last leg of the Tour de France. I call it *The Zone*.

It's that special place that only winners inhabit—where there is no past and no future, only the exhilaration of the moment, of going all out. It makes no difference whether it's an international athletic competition or exceeding your monthly sales quota. Being in The Zone means doing more than you or anyone else thought possible.

Getting there is all a matter of *mental* training, which you're about to acquire.

When you set a goal for yourself or your organization, you're creating a competitive situation. It's similar to an athletic event, because success depends on your ability to combine physical or technical skill with mental process *in a stressful environment.* Although you may be trained to execute certain skills impeccably, your mind must give you the power to perform flawlessly during the heat of competition. At the world-class level in any field, it truly is *mind* over muscle, *mind* over competition, *mind* over everything.

During my years serving on the United States Olympic Committee's Sports Medicine Council, we discovered that American athletes were falling behind those of Europe and Asia in the application of mental training to ensure high performance. When we asked our athletes how much time they spent physically training, the typical answer ranged from two to six hours per day and usually from five to seven days per week. But when we asked how much time they spent training mentally, they responded with bewilderment. Some said they engaged in mental drills of one sort or another, especially just before a competition. Others had tried various relaxation programs, but they usually gave up after a few weeks when nothing remarkable happened.

Yet when asked how important they believe psychological factors are in determining the outcome of the competition, elite athletes generally concluded that once they are in physical condition, *70 to 90 percent of the outcome is based on psychological factors*!

For too long, the emphasis in sports, business, and education has been on physical or technical prowess, rather than on mental skills. We now know that outstanding accomplishment depends upon effective self-management and total self-mastery. In short, no one is born into The Zone, with the mind-set of a champion. But, like any other skill, it can be learned and practiced.

Desire + Action = Motivation

First and foremost, champions in every sport and in every industry are driven by a burning *desire* to succeed. Lee Iacocca called it "fire in the belly." It's the internal force that drives you to peak performance.

That burning desire isn't created by pep talks, bonuses, or any other external notion. The drive to win is motivated from the inside out.

By definition, motivation is *motive in action*. Champions like Greg LeMond know how to transform their aspirations into actions in the real world. At some point in their lives, not always early, they saw something they really wanted to accomplish. They saw it, vaguely and nonspecifically at first. Then they began to think about it, to consider it, to get to know it, to examine it, study it, try it, fail at it, succeed at it, get knowledge about it, field-test it, get coached in it, develop skills in it, and as the concept took shape, it also took root, and like the seedling of a redwood tree, the motive—the goal—is pushed upward through the earth, through bedrock, up through mountains of doubt, skyward, tolerating no distraction or obstacle in the way.

Ray Kroc, who built McDonald's restaurants into a worldwide empire, was in his fifties and selling milk-shake machines for a living when he visited the original McDonald's drive-in restaurant in Riverside, California. He drove up early one morning, before the place opened, and saw customers forming a line outside. He also saw an idea whose time had come, and *nothing* could stop him from turning that idea into reality.

At around the same time, and not many miles away, Walt Disney wanted to build a theme park in Orange County. Of course, they didn't call it a theme park in those days. They didn't know what to call it. Nobody thought it would work. None of the banks wanted to put any money into Disneyland.

That hardly stopped Disney, because champions know where they are and they see where they want to go. They dominate and focus their thoughts and energy on the desired result, and they move toward it. They are propelled by desire, not compelled by fear.

The Four Great Fears

Fear is a powerful negative motivator. We all know of managers who resort to threats, power plays, and punishment in the mistaken idea that it is the fastest way to meet their goals. Even some very successful individuals have operated this way. Thomas J. Watson, Jr., the former CEO of IBM, believed that "the best way to motivate people is to pit them against one another."[1] But in the long run, the use of fear is counterproductive. Rather than enhancing motivation, its effect is to stagnate or paralyze the will to achieve.

Unfortunately, you don't need an overbearing boss for fear to become part of your life. Fear can become internalized. Through fear, you can put "The Drive to Win" in neutral (or reverse) all by yourself.

For many people, there are four clearly defined categories of fear.

First, there's the *Fear of Catastrophic Danger,* which is an automatic, reflexive instinct. This fear causes us to react to what we consider life-threatening confrontations, with the Fight or Flight Syndrome. When we feel threatened by an aggressor, we either defend ourselves by attacking our adversary, or we try to escape harm's way by running in the opposite direction or hiding. Unfortunately, most of us tend to overreact to what's happening. We flare to anger quickly and become defensive in situations that call for calmness and reason. Our instinctive emotions are those we have inherited from a world where we were either hunting *for* food or hunted *as* food!

The best way to overcome the built-in fear of danger and catastrophic loss is knowledge. Get the facts of the situation, and act accordingly. Fear dissipates and often disappears with knowledge and action.

A second major fear—although few people may be willing to admit it—is the *Fear of Change*. Although our Declaration of Independence created a revolution with the phrase "All men are created equal," this phrase seems to have degenerated into, all people are entitled to equal results. Workers punch in at nine A.M. and begin their countdown to five P.M. For too many managers and employees alike, the job is seen as an interruption between weekends.

It seems to me that there's too much talk about the Common Man or Woman. This can lead to a kind of cult worship of mediocrity. And the only redeeming feature about embracing mediocrity is that you never have an off day. Just nice, steady mediocrity.

But think about it. When you have legal problems, you want an uncommon attorney. When you invest your hard-earned life savings, you want an uncommon money manager. If your car breaks down, you want an uncommonly good mechanic. And when you're not feeling well, you certainly want an uncommon doctor. I've never met a mom or dad who did not want his or her kids to grow up to be uncommon men and women.

Today, being a champion requires the ability to embrace change. For many, change represents a threat to the status quo.

For you, let it represent unlimited opportunity. Don't become so well-adapted to a specific set of circumstances that you can't change when conditions begin to fluctuate. Otherwise, you might find yourself going the way of the dinosaurs—or the American automobile industry.

A third fear, which I've studied for many years, is often difficult to recognize. It's the *Fear of Success*. Basically, the fear of success is an expression of guilt associated with our natural desire for self-gratification.

Suppose you're a tremendously successful, world-class champion way out in front of the pack. Think of the guilt! You've outdistanced your peer group and you've gotten out of your comfort zones. You've got to bear the envy and criticism of false friends. You have to justify to yourself that you really deserve all this.

One of my friends and mentors is Dr. Bruce Ogilvie, acknowledged pioneer and father of sports psychology in the United States. In the nearly four decades since he entered the unexplored arena of the mind-set of champions, he has studied nearly twelve thousand of the world's finest athletes. Dr. Ogilvie discovered in his research that one of the greatest inhibitors to high performance is the fear of success syndrome. In business and in personal life, it sometimes remains hidden. But in athletes he saw it clearly.

While working with a young pole-vaulter at Stanford, who was equaling the National Collegiate Athletic Association (NCAA) record in practice, he observed that after two years the vaulter never scored a single point in competition. Ogilvie eventually discovered that the young man was terrified, subconsciously, that if he achieved his goals and dreams, he'd have to meet the expectations of others for the rest of his life. And he found that unbearable.

In another case, a twenty-year-old right-handed pitcher in baseball had dominated hitters in the Triple-A minor leagues, driving them off the plate with a wicked breaking ball and smoking them with a fastball. In late summer he was called up to the majors and flopped. He couldn't get the ball over the plate and when he did, he got hit hard. In his first interview with Dr. Ogilvie, the kid kept saying, "How did I get here? I don't belong here. How can I pitch to somebody like Mike Schmidt? He's my hero."

Bruce Ogilvie, realizing he was dealing with a classic fear-of-success case, observed that the young athlete was so in awe at being in the major leagues, there was no way he could let himself succeed. To help, Ogilvie focused on the pitcher's strengths, going over and over all that he'd accomplished in order to reach the major leagues. At the same time, he worked with the veterans on the team to build a positive support structure for the newcomer. The older players would come by and say, "Glad you're here, kid, we really need you," which the players were happy to do because they did need him. The coach started putting him in, in late innings, when the game was lost or won. He did well and built up his confidence. He worked his way back into the starting rotation and became a success.

During the last thirty years, I have worked with people from all walks of life—famous and unknown. For most of them, their greatest fear is the *Fear of Failure,* which is really a *fear of rejection.*

We all have a natural aversion to being embarrassed or made a fool of in the presence of others. More than any other factor, this fear of what might happen, not what *will* happen, holds us back and causes us to procrastinate. We permit ourselves to fail by default rather than face the risks of success.

What Makes a Winner?

Champions don't shrink from risk. Champions know that the greatest risk is doing nothing, and that real security derives from constantly testing your potential. The Gallup organization, one of our most reliable polling firms, recently investigated the "success-oriented personality," probing the attitudes and traits of fifteen hundred prominent individuals selected at random from *Who's Who in America*. The results were very illuminating.

The three most important traits of a winner were:

- *Common sense,* or the ability to simplify complex subjects by getting right to the core of what really matters.

- *Knowing your field*, both through hands-on experience and the advice of other people.

- *Self-reliance*, which means more than just feeling good about yourself. It means taking definitive action to get things moving in your life.

I had the good fortune to learn about self-reliance early in life. My father had gone overseas in World War II. I was nine, and the eldest boy in the family. There was an army antiaircraft gun emplacement near our home in San Diego. The soldiers stationed there would make friends with us to occupy their lonely extra hours, and they would give us military souvenirs. I got a camouflaged army helmet, a gun belt, and a canteen for drinking water. In return, I'd bring them candy, magazines, and invite them to our house for some home cooking, such as it was. We didn't have any money and couldn't afford much food, but we never went to bed hungry and what few clothes we had my mom always helped keep clean.

I'll never forget one day when one of my soldier friends said, "I want to take you fishing in a boat, Sunday, at five A.M." I replied, barely able to keep my feet on the ground, "Oh, wow! I'd love to go. I've never even been near a boat. I've always fished off the bridge, or the pier, or the rocks and just watched the boats heading out in the ocean. But I've always dreamed of going fishing on a boat. Oh, thank you. I'll ask my mom if you can come over for dinner next Saturday.''

I was so excited I went to bed with my clothes and tennis shoes on, so I'd be sure not to be late. I lay in my bed, unable to sleep, counting big sea bass and barracuda that I imagined were swimming on the ceiling. At three A.M. I sneaked out of my bedroom window, got my tackle box all set with extra hooks and leaders, oiled my fishing reel, packed two peanut butter and jelly sandwiches, and at four A.M. I was ready to go with my fishing pole, my tackle box, my lunch, and my enthusiasm— sitting on the curb in front of my house, waiting in the dark for my friend the soldier.

But he never showed.

That probably was a pivotal point in my life in terms of self-reliance.

Instead of being either cynical or self-pitying, crawling back into bed and sulking, or getting upset and telling my mom, my sister, my brother, and my friends that this guy never showed, that he broke his promise—I went to a swap meet at the local drive-in movie lot and spent all of my lawn-mowing earnings on a patched-up, one-man rubber life raft I had seen there the week before. I blew air into it, which took me until almost noon, carried it on my head with my gear in it like a safari native, and pretended I was launching a marvelous cabin cruiser in the ocean. I paddled out in the bay, caught some fish, ate my sandwiches, drank punch out of the army canteen, and had one of the most marvelous days of my life. It was an all-time high.

When I look back on that day—and I often do—I always ponder what I learned, even at the tender age of nine. First I learned that when the fish are biting, no problem in the world is big enough to be remembered. And the fish did bite that afternoon! Second, my soldier friend taught me that having only good intentions doesn't cut it. He wanted to take me, he thought about taking me, he may have even been planning to take me before his alarm clock did or didn't go off, but, because it wasn't his burning desire, he set no real goals to do it—and he didn't show.

For me, however, going fishing that day was my magnificent obsession and I immediately began setting goals to make my desire a reality. I could have let disappointment defeat me. I could have just gone home, telling myself, "You wanted to go fishing, but the soldier didn't come, so that's that." Instead, something told me that you can't win with desire only. You need to break that desire down into smaller parts and reach your main goal by what I call the "stair-step" method.

The Stair-Step Method

Not since the legendary feats of Mildred "Babe" Didrickson in the 1930s and 1940s has there been another female athlete with the all-around ability of Jackie Joyner-Kersee. She is in a class by herself. In both the summer Olympics of 1988 in Seoul, Korea and in the 1992 Olympics in Barcelona, Spain, she won gold medals in the heptathlon. This is a grueling seven-event competition, spread over two days. It requires speed, strength, and stamina.

Jackie Joyner-Kersee has all of these. No one in the world really challenged her in either Olympics. She took the heptathlon to a new and lofty level.

Part of her success is due to the special relationship she shares with her husband and coach, Bob Kersee. They employ the stair-step method of achievement used by many great champions in every field. Stair-stepping means taking a big goal and breaking it down into smaller components. In Jackie's case, the overall goal was to win the heptathlon competition and break her own world record. The smaller components were the individual performances she needed in each event to achieve the major goal.

For example, in 1992, Jackie high-jumped six feet, three and one quarter inches and ran the 100-meter dash in 12.85 seconds. These were on target with her overall goal. However, in the shot put, she performed five feet short of her stair-step target. Although the shot put prevented her from another world record, she won the gold medal easily, thrilling the stadium crowds with her amazing skills and endurance.

Jackie Joyner-Kersee savors her victories, but is never one to rest on her laurels. She is taking her experience in the shot put in Barcelona and setting new stair-step goals to increase her strength in that and other events, so that she can look toward breaking her own world record in future competition.

By setting lower-level goals—ones that are measurable and *relatively* easier to reach—it's easier to make corrections when you get off target. If you tried to eat an entire steak in one mouthful, you'd choke. But by cutting it into smaller, bite-sized pieces it's digestible and enjoyable. Achieving goals step by step also builds your confidence: While smaller, the successes are experienced more often. This provides the positive feedback and reinforcement necessary for achieving any big goal.

In a business setting, the power of this approach is exemplified by a statistician and management consultant named Dr. W. Edwards Deming.

Perhaps, like many people in this country, you've never heard of Dr. Deming. His management philosophy, particularly regarding manufacturing, was based on keeping close track of progress and making continuous small improvements. Although he was largely a prophet without honor in his own country, beginning in the 1950s his ideas were wholeheartedly embraced by the Japanese. It's no exaggeration to say that the success of the Japanese auto industry derives directly from the thinking of Ed Deming. The Deming Prize for Quality is still the most prestigious award possible for any Japanese company. The winner is announced on a national television show, just like the Oscars.

But even when he was considered a hero in Japan, Deming was ignored by the Big Three in Detroit.

Finally, around 1980, Donald E. Petersen, now CEO of Ford, happened to watch a TV documentary about the success of the Japanese car industry, in which Dr. Deming was prominently featured. Petersen immediately met with Deming and began to introduce the notions of team-building and the close monitoring of continuous small improvements. These ideas played a prominent role in the design and manufacture of the Ford Taurus, one of the best American cars in the past twenty years.[2]

Maximum success is built upon minigoals. Any goal can be achieved, but first it must be broken down into a series of subgoals. Each smaller goal should lead you, one day at a time, to your larger life goal. With our Olympic champions, we described this process using a four-part terminology: *define, outline, time-frame*, and *claim*.

By *defining* each major goal in writing, it becomes a clear mission statement and has the authority of a legal contract.

By *outlining* each major goal in the form of stair-steps, it becomes focused, less intimidating, and more easily scheduled into your daily and weekly routine.

The *time-frame* we have found most effective is "The Magic of Ninety Days," or what I call the length of a season, because each major athletic season lasts about ninety days. Similarly, a corporate interim financial report appears quarterly, representing ninety days of earnings. There is a natural rhythm and a cycle to this length of time. The magic of ninety days is that you can manage this period effectively by planning weekly and daily activities toward a "winning season."

In short, once you've broken your major goals into ninety-day projects, you can tame them—and *claim* them!

Nobody Else Is Going to Take You Fishing

When Greg LeMond began seriously training for the 1990 Tour de France, there were many who criticized him for missing all the bicycle racing classics in the spring. He was just coming off a serious bout of viral flu. With only ninety days of serious training before the event, his critics wrote him off as having no chance to repeat his amazing success of the year before.

But, coming from far behind, LeMond stair-stepped his way through the grueling twenty-one-stage race, not winning a single stage during the twenty-two-day period, but making history on the final day as he silenced his detractors with another impossible Tour de France victory in 1990. Unlike his spectacular win in 1989, LeMond didn't burst across the finish line in Paris to win in eight seconds. By breaking the race into minigoals, he won by strategy, tactics and bite-size efforts. Ignoring what others did or thought or said, LeMond formulated his own approach, implemented it, and followed it through to victory.

As a nine-year-old kid, I had to learn that other people weren't going to take me fishing. I had to take myself and the same is true for you.

Don't wait for that miracle or that break or "the right time." Today is your day. Choose how you will spend it, and do the same with every other day of the rest of your life. You are in charge of causing your results. Don't put it off. Don't put success on lay-away. Don't sit staring at that TV screen letting your mind go blank while you repeat the procrastinator's motto: *I think I can, I think I could; I think I may, I think I should; I think I might, I think I will; I think I better think more still.* Stop rationalizing, get out of your chair, and start doing!

For starters, ask yourself some hard questions:

- Are you dissatisfied with the status quo?

- What do you have to change in order to move toward where you want to be?

- Which fears do you need to conquer? Do you fear change? Do you fear failure? Do you fear success?

Forget the advice of all those experts, associates, friends, and relatives who tell you you can't possibly have what you want. Remember, producer Irving Thalberg strongly advised Louis B. Mayer against buying the rights to *Gone With the Wind* because no Civil War picture had ever made a nickel. No producer in modern times expected a quaint movie adapted from a play like *Driving Miss Daisy* to last a full week in the shoot-to-kill box office wars. And when a slightly out-of-shape Greg LeMond showed up in Europe for the Tour de France in 1990, the headlines blared, HE'S FAT AND HE'S FINISHED.

Well, LeMond(e) in French means the world. And that's what he's got at his feet!

CHAPTER TWO

Paying the Price

The entry fee to success
Why working hard isn't enough
When you've paid the price, you expect the gold
Seven rules for winners, and how to apply them
Recognizing your moment of truth
How to get the best seat in the house

The Entry Fee to Success

In Chapter One, I asked you to relive Greg LeMond's spectacular accomplishments in the Tour de France. It was a story that had special significance for me. While I'm certainly no Greg LeMond, I did happen to get one of my earliest lessons about commitment aboard a bicycle. Maybe you did, too.

Can you remember when you got your first two-wheeler? It's an experience many people can instantly recall. I'll never forget when I got a bicycle for Christmas. My whole family stood on the lawn watching me try to take my first ride. On that day, I discovered why commitment is definitely like riding a bicycle.

First, you must believe that a machine that can't even stand by itself will transport you safely. Of course, you've seen it work for others, but now you've got to convince yourself that this form of success can actually happen to you.

Second, you must let go of all forms of support and balance yourself with the sheer force of momentum created by your own strength.

Third, you have to lean into curves. This becomes easy enough after a while, but at the beginning the natural tendency is to incline yourself away from what appears to be a potentially dangerous situation. You've got to realize that the best way to avoid falling doesn't involve simply staying as far as possible from the ground.

Fourth, you can coast for a while, but you won't get far if you don't keep pedaling! The lesson there, I'm sure, is self-evident.

Last, you've got to get up and try again after you've fallen off the bicycle. Kids will fall any number of times, but they'll almost never say, "I quit. I'm not willing to risk falling again. Forget bicycling, I'd rather just walk." Kids rarely attach any significance to even dozens of falls or failures. It's just part of the price they gladly pay for that marvelous experience of flying down the street under their own power.

This commitment to "paying the price" is a key quality in the mind of a champion. You could even say that if success has an entry fee, the cost is *total commitment*.

Why Working Hard Isn't Enough

Commitment is probably even more important in work and career than it is in athletics, because when you're rushing to finish a sales projection or create a new business plan, there are no coaches or cheering crowds to get your adrenaline flowing. The energy has to come from within yourself. You have to say, "This is a major priority in my life. I want to be good at this, and I'm going to do everything in my power to do this as well as I possibly can."

It's tempting to think that commitment is just another word

for "working hard." But unfortunately, it isn't quite that simple. Statistics show that Americans are working harder than ever. The massive entrance of women into the work force, and the prevalence of two-career families, means that we're putting in an enormous number of working hours per household. In terms of productivity, too, America still leads the world. But those statistics are really just numbers on a page.

What's more difficult to measure is the way you *feel* about your work, and *how much of yourself* you really put into it. There may not be numbers to back this up, but there's a sense that the level of commitment is falling for many people in all sectors of the American economy.

There are many reasons for this, as a recent article in *The Wall Street Journal* discussed.[1] It pointed out that layoffs, transfers, and plant closings have left both managers and blue-collar workers feeling alienated from their companies. People are unwilling to invest themselves wholeheartedly in their work when there's no guarantee that they'll even *be* working next week or next month. It's safer for some to start thinking of a job simply as what you do between weekends. When you're thinking like that, your work isn't really *you*—it's just what you do in order to get somebody to sign your paychecks.

As the *Journal* article suggests, it doesn't have to be that way. When American workers are given the opportunities and the incentives to put themselves into their work in a meaningful way, they respond. Teams of workers at a company called Cincinnati Milacron built a high-tech, computer-controlled lathe virtually without direct management supervision. The hourly workers were not subject to time cards, yet absenteeism was almost nonexistent. They assembled the lathe, prepared the electronic controls, wired it, installed it, and instructed customers in its use. These workers were freed of all responsibilities except one: the commitment to do their best.

When American Olympic hopefuls are given written tests,

it certainly isn't to test their knowledge of the sports in which they'll be participating. The tests are psychological inventories designed to reveal the athletes' level of commitment. It's been proven that those who "want it more" will be willing to train harder and longer, and those who are able to delay immediate pleasure for long-term results will ultimately demonstrate the highest performance. Conversely, as the commitment score on the psychological tests decreased, the athletes' performance level decreased proportionately. This was true for all sports from marathon runners to badminton players, from platform divers to ice hockey players.

How would you rate *your* commitment to achieving your career goals? It's something that can't be measured simply in terms of hours worked or dollars earned. Quite simply, it's a question of how much you "want it."

If the commitment is there, the achievements will follow. Attaining top-level results may require some time, but you can make *the commitment* starting right now.

When You've Paid the Price, You Expect the Gold

The Olympic champion Mary Lou Retton is a good illustration of the way, slowly but surely, achievements grow out of commitment.

Mary Lou wasn't born a classic gymnast. She wasn't graceful. She didn't have the movements of a ballet dancer. She was just four feet nine inches tall, with a compact, muscular body. She looked more like a sprinter than a potential gymnastics star.

Because she was totally committed, she didn't fear paying the price of success. She said, "I knew I wouldn't look graceful in floor exercises, or doing those piqué turns and ballerina moves. But I was a good sprinter and I had a lot of power and explosiveness. So I could do some things some of the other girls couldn't do.''

By the age of fourteen she was West Virginia State Champion, and winning gymnastic meets throughout the world. But as young as she was, she was mature enough to realize she needed to do much more.

''I needed someone pushing me,'' she said. ''I needed some other girls around me who were shooting for the same goal I was.''

So, at a time when most teenagers are thinking about anything but commitment, Mary Lou Retton made an enormous sacrifice. She left the comfort of her home in Fairmont, West Virginia, and moved to Houston, into the home of a family she didn't know, just for the opportunity to train under one of the world's greatest, but most demanding, gymnastic coaches, Bela Karolyi.

While other kids were watching TV, going to a movie, hanging out with friends, and going on trips, she was practicing four hours a day, seven days a week. Karolyi changed everything Mary Lou had been doing for eight years, from the way she tumbled to the way she ate. As the Olympic games drew nearer, she described her day this way. ''An eight o'clock workout, then to school, back to the gym for four more hours of work, then homework, then bed.''

A grind? To be sure. Fun? Not much. Then why? Because winners work at doing things the rest of the population won't even consider trying. She may not have enjoyed the routine, but she loved the sport, the challenge, and the dream.

Then, just a few weeks before the summer games, her right knee suddenly locked. Fragments of torn cartilage had broken loose and become wedged in the knee joint. Less than ten days after orthoscopic surgery, she was back in the gym for a full workout. There was no time to lose, only time to get ready to win. She hadn't prepared for so many years just to let the payoff get away. *Commitment* kept her going.

In her final event, the vault, Mary Lou needed a 9.95, a near perfect performance, to tie the Romanian favorite for the gold medal. One writer described her effort this way: "She raced down the line, sprang off the vault, twisted at high altitude. and landed as still as a dropped bar of lead, yet as soft as a springtime butterfly."

She scored a perfect ten, the ultimate. But to the surprise and awe of spectators, officials, and participants, she went ahead and executed the optional second vault.

Incredibly, the result was the same again, a perfect ten!

The only one not surprised was Mary Lou Retton. She was ready to enter the winner's circle, because she knew she'd paid the price.[2]

Paying the price of success, for most of us, seems like paying the United States' national debt. It appears overwhelming for us to invest in ourselves the amount of time and effort required for peak performance. Too often, we believe our own physical and environmental limitations are unique and much greater than those of gifted champions.

Gail's problems surfaced in 1988, her last year at UCLA. She began suffering from an agonizing series of physical problems. She had migraine headaches, partial blindness, memory loss, and convulsions. Her weight increased and declined dramatically, and she had difficulty sleeping. For nearly two years she lived in constant pain and the doctors she consulted couldn't tell her why.

Finally, in 1990, a physician diagnosed her illness as Graves' disease, the thyroid condition that also afflicts George and Barbara Bush, although *much* less severely in each of their cases. If Gail's disease had gone untreated for two more weeks, doctors say it may have resulted in cancer.

The initial treatment called for radiation and chemotherapy.

Gail's feet began to swell and blister and her skin began to crack and peel. The pain was so great she couldn't walk. When she tried to crawl, the skin rubbed off her knees. A doctor told her that if she had attempted to walk for even two more days, her feet might have had to be amputated to save her life. This occurred a little more than a year prior to the 1992 Olympic Games in Barcelona. Think back to the summer before the 1992 Olympics. Where were you? What was happening in your life at that time?

In March of 1991, Gail's therapy was changed and she began to improve. Most of us would have been happy to be alive or to have feet to put into our shoes. Gail took a stationary bike out to the track and peddled relentlessly while her teammates sprinted and worked out around her. Within a month, she was able to walk, in sweat socks, around the UCLA track.

A few months later, Gail was running competitively. A year later, Gail Devers was at the Olympics in Barcelona. She was not the favorite in the 100-meter dash. She won the gold in the fastest time of her career.

Gail Devers is a living testimony of the agony of defeat and the thrill of victory. It seemed inconceivable that her incredible comeback could be marred by a setback in her next event, the hurdles. Heading for a certain second gold-medal performance, well ahead of her competitors, Gail's speed was so great that she hit the last hurdle, plunged to the ground, and crawled across the finish line. The world watched in silent disbelief.

The postrace interview showed the grace typical of Gail Devers. She was philosophical and unruffled. She was upbeat and content. She said it was one of those things that happen that you have to take in stride. As Gail put it, "Going through what I've gone through, there's no obstacle I can't overcome."

No wooden hurdle will ever stand in Gail Devers's way. Most of our hurdles in life are self-imposed limitations that can be overcome if we never, ever give up on ourselves.

Seven Rules for Winners, and How to Apply Them

How can you apply the success principles of an Olympic gymnast to your own life? It's easier than you think, because there are in fact certain basic rules that all winners follow, whether it's in the sports arena or the corporate boardroom. Make them your rules, too.

THE SEVEN RULES FOR WINNERS

Rule 1: Be proactive and preventive about your physical health.

You have received a body. You may like it or hate it, but it will be yours for the duration. Take responsibility for it. Treat your body like a spacecraft, not like a used car that you drive around, hoping you won't have to spend much on maintenance.

Your physical well-being is your most precious gift, yet it's something that many people can't fully appreciate until they lose it. Start taking care of your health by having a complete physical, and continue doing so annually. Be aware also of the health history and current status of your close relatives. Their experiences, combined with your own health record, will reveal lifestyle changes you may need to make.

Then, with your doctor's permission, formulate an exercise program, and stick to it. Make it fun! For me, that means swimming, going for a long, fast-paced walk with my dog, and gardening. One hour of steady, intense gardening can burn as many as four hundred calories and give my arms and legs a real workout. I also enjoy playing badminton with my wife in our backyard. Exercise does not have to be a workout. It can be a play-at-home project.

Rule 2: View life as a continuous learning experience.

You are enrolled in a full-time informal school called life. Each day in this school you will have the opportunity to learn new lessons, some of which you may enjoy a great deal—and some you may enjoy not at all. But see to it that these learning experiences never end. Think of success as a process that you want to continue, not a status that you reach once and for all.

People who fail to do this can reach a certain comfort zone of security, where they stop growing and reaching. Salespeople who have been working hard for years at a forty-thousand-dollar annual income level finally break through to the seventy-five-thousand a year level. They settle in, enjoying the country club and the good life, and make just enough calls to stay at that level. Their client base degenerates while they fail to regenerate. They rest on their laurels, and sooner or later, they get knocked off their perch.

Bill Lear was a good example of an individual who never let success stop him from seeking out new challenges. Lear was a lifelong tinkerer and inventor in the classic American mode of Henry Ford and Thomas Edison. He made a fortune with a navigational aid for airplanes called the Learoscope, and later branched out into stereo systems and communications satellites. He was past sixty when he marketed the Learjet, and it quickly became the ultimate business aircraft. At sixty-five, Lear sold his business and tried retirement, but the life of an idle multimillionaire quickly lost its luster. Even when he knew he was dying of leukemia, he kept working at his laboratory in Reno, Nevada, on projects ranging from jet planes to steam engines. Lear was referring to one of those projects when he spoke his last words to his colleagues. They were, "Finish it? You bet we'll finish it!"[3]

Rule 3: You get what you pay for.

This rule is perhaps the most neglected one of all, and failing to recognize its importance is what causes most people to realize only a fraction of their potential.

You get what you pay for means, metaphorically, that you've got to put in the effort, the hours, or even the years that are required to master a skill.

Let's examine just what that means for world-class athletes.

Competing at the Olympic level requires hours of training every day—and that's just to qualify, not to win. To prepare for the actual games, you need to make a full-time, total commitment at least four years prior to the actual event. That means you're training for the next Olympiad while a current Olympiad is being staged. The athletes work a minimum of eight hours per day, six and a half days a week. That's fifty hours per week of practice. With days off for competition, travel, and recovering from injuries, they average fifty weeks a year of practice, or a total of twenty-five hundred hours per year.

In other words, assuming that you've reached the world-class level at your particular skill, it still takes another ten thousand hours of training and practice, just for the privilege of walking around the stadium track with your teammates at the Olympic opening ceremonies.

Of course, there are exceptions to the rule—like Jennifer Capriati, one of the most sensational new tennis stars of the 1990s. She started swinging a tennis racket at the age of three, but it wasn't until the ripe old age of eleven that she won her first tournament. She's the youngest person ever to turn professional in the history of the sport—shortly before her fourteenth birthday. And she's been setting records ever since.

Another exception, this time from the business world, is Bill Gates, founder of Microsoft. Gates became interested in computers while still in grade school in Seattle, and one summer he earned more than four thousand dollars for programming the school schedules. Later, he and a partner earned twenty thousand dollars for using a computer to analyze Seattle traffic patterns. Bill Gates was all of fifteen!

While serving as a congressional page in Washington, he

witnessed the 1972 presidential election campaign between Nixon and McGovern from up close. When Senator McGovern dropped Senator Thomas Eagleton as his running mate, Gates bought the suddenly obsolete campaign buttons for five cents each—and soon sold them as historical memorabilia for as much as twenty-five dollars apiece.[4]

I guess it's no surprise that Gates was recently listed by *Forbes* magazine as the second richest person in the United States.

But remember: Bill Gates and Jennifer Capriati are exceptions. They combined great talent with opportunity, and they gained early success. Far more typical of world-class achievers was Walter Chrysler, who was already an accomplished locomotive mechanic when, in 1905, he purchased an expensive automobile with borrowed money. He drove the new car to a garage and proceeded to take it apart. Then he put it back together again. In fact, Chrysler took the car apart and put it together somewhere between forty and fifty times. Once he knew that he could virtually assemble the machine blindfolded, he was also satisfied that he could build a better car.[5]

In other words, Walter Chrysler knew that he had paid the price. And you get what you pay for.

Rule 4: View mistakes as corrective feedback to get you back on track.

There are no mistakes or failures, only lessons. Growth is a process of gaining knowledge, of trial and error, and of courageous experimentation. The failed attempts can be as much a part of the success process as the attempt that finally succeeds.

Rejection and guilt are tied deeply to failure. The experience of a failure, which results in feelings of disappointment, is actually like being told to go stand in a corner because you've been a bad boy or naughty girl. People equate failure with the worst of punishments, which is the fear of peer rejection or a loved one's disapproval. We know of hundreds of cases of individuals who come from bankruptcy back to success, but the emotional injuries can be the most difficult to heal. To succeed, you've got to develop the sense of basic self-worth that will overcome the inevitable mistakes and setbacks.

Ray Kroc used to say, "Mistakes are painful when they happen . . . but years later a collection of mistakes is called experience."

If you feel you've made some mistakes or taken some wrong turns in your career, consider the case of a man named Gerald Fralick. He felt the same way in 1962, when he was flipping hamburgers at a White Castle for the minimum wage. This didn't seem to be leading anywhere, so he decided to try selling life insurance instead.[6]

Why life insurance? Twelve years later, after he'd sold more than fifty-million-dollars'-worth of policies, Fralick explained it like this to *The Miami Herald*: "It was because I thought that's what you did when you had failed at everything else."

Rule 5: Set your own internal standards for success.

Don't compare yourself to others. Competition should be viewed as a way to maintain excellence, to keep yourself performing up to your own potential. Though we're all tempted to compare ourselves with someone else, the happiest people in life know they don't really compete against others. Their success comes from doing their best, based on their unique skills and goals.

The fact is, other individuals are merely mirrors of what you see in yourself. You can't love or hate something about another person unless it reflects something you love or hate about yourself. Choose role models you can learn the most from, not those whose appearance you like the most. The success of others has little to do with your personal success. True success is not measured by what others may say or accomplish.

Instead of achieving or performing to impress the world or

your peers, seek to do something that you love, something that is excellent, and beneficial. You need no one else to measure you or your skill. Your main audience should be your own self-respect.

Willie Davis, the great defensive end of the Green Bay Packers in the Vince Lombardi era, expressed this very well. When he was asked how he maintained his intensity game after game, he answered: "I've got to play that way, because I've got to live with myself."

Willie Davis simply couldn't face looking in the mirror each morning if he felt that he'd given less than his best. Once you've learned to challenge yourself that deeply, with your own personal standards, you've already taken one of the biggest steps toward achieving your goals. In a real sense, you've already succeeded. It's just a matter of time before the rest of the world finds out.

Rule 6: The choice is yours—so choose to win.

What you make of your life is up to you. You have all the tools and resources you need. What you do with them is your decision. The choice is yours. And it's never too late to get in the game.

Consider Sister Mary Martin Weaver, a Catholic nun, who took up athletics many years ago—at the age of fifty-five. She has won forty-four gold, silver, and bronze medals in a variety of events, including the five-thousand-meter race walk, snowshoe racing, speed and figure skating, basketball free throws, shotput, and ice hockey!

At an age when some people are going for the gold medal in napping, Sister Mary has become a fixture at the Rocky Mountain Senior Games and the U.S. National Senior Olympics.

"People have gotten flabby," she says, "and I don't mean just physically. Anything that's too much, people just don't want to do. But there are no rewards in anything unless you try. Age should never be a barrier to full participation in life. What's most important is to enjoy life to its fullest, to do things for and with others, and never, ever be afraid to stretch your limits. Choose to win!''[7]

Rule 7: Keep training and gaining—without complaining.

Losers like to engage in pleasurable activities with no particular result in mind. We call this *instant gratification*. Winners choose activities that will give them long-term positive results. That's *delayed gratification*.

Delayed gratification is, perhaps, the most difficult rule to teach people in America today, but it really is what separates champions from also-rans.

Here's what golfing legend Lee Trevino told my friend and colleague Dr. Doris Lee McCoy in an interview:

> People often tell me, ''You're the luckiest guy in the world. I wish I could do what you do.'' Well, they don't realize it, but they probably could. But you've got to be willing to sacrifice, whether it's as a computer operator or a professional golfer. You have to devote every spare moment to the field you've chosen.
>
> Of course, that means there are lots of things you're not going to be able to do, and some of those might be things you enjoy. Maybe you won't be able to go away on weekends, or go camping or water skiing or whatever. In golf, there are a lot of players with potential, but they won't sacrifice for their goal. They'd rather quit practicing at 2:00 in the afternoon and go have a beer with the gang.[8]

Is there a lesson to be drawn from the fact that sales of reclining chairs, including those designed for the office, are at an all-time high?[9] If Lee Trevino owns a reclining chair, he most certainly keeps it far away from the golf course. Trevino says: ''I learned a long time ago that the best psychology in golf is to hit so many balls that your hands get blistered and calloused. If there's sunlight, there are golf balls to be hit! That's the best psychology I could ever tell anybody.''

Lee Trevino is the third all-time money winner in the history of professional golf.

Recognizing Your Moment of Truth

You can use the seven rules we've described to convert your desire to win into a *total commitment* to win, by paying the price of long-term success.

Earlier in this chapter, I told you about Mary Lou Retton's decision to take the ultimate risk in her young career during the Olympic games. After she scored a perfect ten in the vault, which had never been done by an American in Olympic competition, she went ahead and executed the optional second vault, knowing she could make a mistake, a slip, a slight distraction, or a minor error, and, under the tough rules, lose her first ten and lose it all. Again she scored a perfect ten. For her that was the moment of truth.

For most of us, this moment of truth, this magnificent turning point in our lives, is not so dramatic or satisfying or even recognizable. But recognize it or not, you will have a moment of truth that can alter the course of your life forever, if only you'll catch it and make the most of it.

What has been your moment of truth so far? What has happened in your life that seems to point the way toward what you hope to achieve?

Baseball legend Mike Schmidt grew up in a quiet, tree-lined neighborhood in Dayton, Ohio. His moment of truth came early. At the time, he didn't even know what hit him.

At the age of five he climbed a tree in his backyard and grabbed a four-thousand-volt power line. Knocked unconscious by the shock, he fell to the ground, and the impact restarted his heart.

From then on, Mike Schmidt felt like he'd been given a second chance. In an interview with the Pittsburgh *Post Gazette*, Mike Schmidt said that he didn't want to waste the chance he'd been given—and so worked extra hard from then on.

A moment of truth can come in the form of an accident, as it did for Mike Schmidt, or it might be a chance encounter with another person, or it could be something as mundane as reading an article in the newspaper. A moment of truth can be any event, good or bad, positive or negative. The point is, it becomes a turning point when you seize the moment, ask the big questions, and make *the commitment* to convert that moment into an opportunity for altering your own destiny.

Helping you to recognize that moment, and to make that commitment, is the purpose of this chapter. Once you've done that, you can use our seven rules to turn your commitment into success.

How to Get the Best Seat in the House

There's a steep hill in a suburb of Chicago that was an important element in the creation of one of the greatest professional football players of all time, the leading ground gainer in the history of the National Football League.

During the off-season, *every* off-season, he would run up that steep hill. No matter how hot and humid the day might get, regardless of thundershowers or mud, he still charged up that hill over and over again.

Sometimes other players would join him, and even players from other teams throughout the league would race him. After a short time they would quit, totally exhausted. They couldn't believe anyone would be that obsessed with conquering a hill. But he urged them to keep going until they dropped, and even then, he went a few more times. Finally, when he felt he too had had enough, he went *one last time*.

When football season came again, he fought for every yard, every inch. It usually took more than one opponent to bring him down.

And near the end of the games, when victory or defeat was still undecided, that hill would really pay off for Walter Payton of the Chicago Bears. While others faded, he would seem to get stronger.

That he was talented is without question. But all professional players have talent. What Payton also had was that hill. It wasn't fun. It wasn't glamorous. It wasn't publicized. It was, quite simply, his way of *paying the price*.

When you—like Walter Payton, Mary Lou Retton, and Lee Trevino—have paid the price in full, you too can have the best seat in the house.

The one at the top of the hill.

CHAPTER THREE

The Olympian Within

It begins with a dream

Champions are born, losers are "unmade"

For love, not for money

The five fundamentals of self-esteem

The voices of the past

The "unholy trinity"

Perfectionism and protectionism

Self-worth and self-trust

A triple-axle off the merry-go-round

Ten self-affirming beliefs

It Begins with a Dream

You're standing on the highest pedestal, the one in the center. You hear the roar of approval from the crowd. As the first note of the national anthem is played in the Olympic stadium, you feel all the pride and honor that accompanies this moment. Your eyes well up with tears of exhilaration and joy as the Stars and Stripes are raised, signifying that you are the Olympic gold medal winner. Ten thousand hours of preparation for this one triumphant moment in history!

* * *

That dream of an Olympic championship is in the heart of every amateur athlete, just as the World Series or the Super Bowl are the goals of professional baseball and football players. What are *your* dreams? You're probably not a world-class athlete, but surely you have aspirations of your own. Perhaps you imagine a metaphorical gold medal being placed around your neck by the CEO of your company, or by your friends and your family for being the best in the world in your own unique way.

My own dream began many years ago.

It began on Sunday afternoons, when my parents and grandparents would take us to ride the huge merry-go-round (my grandma preferred to call it the carousel) in beautiful Balboa Park near the San Diego Zoo. Dressed in our Sunday best, we would mount those bobbing zebras, stallions, lions, and tigers, and whirl round and round to the music of the antique pipe organ. Surrounded by mirrors and lights, our hearts would pound in anticipation as we stretched and reached out desperately, trying to be the one among all the riders who would grab the gold ring and win another ride.

Since you're probably younger than I am, you may never even have heard of grabbing the gold ring on the merry-go-round. But in the 1930s, 40s, and 50s, if you reached out and caught it, you not only got a free ride—your name was also announced over the loudspeaker and all the other kids and their parents would applaud. And, of course, the kids all wished it could have been them instead of you.

Reflecting back now on my youth, I've come to some realizations. I guess I did think of success and winning as something that you got by reaching *outside* yourself and proving *to others* that you were worthy. Come to think of it, most of my friends also believed that you had to prove, or earn, or win, or perform in some special way, and then you would deserve the gold ring or the Olympic medal.

The approval of others seemed to *precede* feelings of self-confidence and self-worth. You were entitled to feel good about yourself only *after* you performed well. Why did it take me so many years to discover that just the reverse ought to be true?

After devoting most of my lifetime to investigating the wellsprings of personal and professional success, I'm able to make the following statements with great confidence:

- You need to feel love inside yourself before you can offer it to anyone else.

- Your own sense of value determines the quality of your performance. Performance is only a reflection of internal worth, not the measure of it.

- The less you try to impress, the more impressive you are.

- What you show to the world on the outside is a reflection of how you feel on the inside.

Champions Are Born, Losers Are "Unmade"

The key trait shared by athletic champions and winners in every walk of life is the fundamental belief in one's own internal value. If your success depends on external possessions, you'll be subject to constant anxiety. When your peer group cheers one of your accomplishments, you'll feel good for a while, but then you'll wonder if they'll cheer as loudly the next time. If they're critical, you will feel hurt and threatened. The truth is, you can never win if your concept of success depends upon the perfect performance or the placing of a gold medal around your neck.

It's obvious that talent, looks, and other attributes aren't equally distributed among us, but we're all given an abundance of value—more than we could use in several lifetimes. The game of life certainly isn't played on a level playing field for each of us in terms of education, a supportive home life, and other circumstances beyond our control, but I can assure you that you were born with the qualities of a champion. That's what I mean by *value*.

You see, champions are born, but they can be *unmade* by their perceptions and responses. Losers are not born to lose. They're programmed that way by their own perceptions and decisions.

There's a phrase I like to use—The Inner Winner—that describes the kind of person who recognizes his or her internal value, and who is able to use that recognition as the foundation for achieving any goal. The secret of wearing the gold medal around your neck in the external world is that first you must be an Inner Winner. You must recognize that you're already *an Olympian within*.

For Love, Not for Money

Since the end of World War II, but especially during the 1980s, it's been fashionable to invest in art. Many of the art investors were people whose motivation was more strongly financial than it was aesthetic. Everyone had read about Van Gogh paintings selling for millions of dollars. So why not find the *new* Van Goghs, buy their work for a song, and then cash in a few years later?

Buying paintings was just like buying real estate, except that you can't hang real estate over the fireplace of your townhouse.

There's no doubt that some people have made huge profits by investing in art—but many of them were rich to start out with.

Most of the speculators who were looking for the new Van Gogh would have been better off buying old-fashioned piggy banks.

Herbert and Dorothy Vogel never looked at buying art as a shortcut to wealth. But they were fascinated by new painting and sculpture, and they loved talking with the artists who created it. For more than thirty years, the New York City postal clerk and his wife, who worked in the Brooklyn Public Library, sought out unknown artists and bought pieces that they found interesting or beautiful. They never sold anything. Over the years, the Vogels' one-bedroom Manhattan apartment became literally filled to overflowing, with their collection of twenty-five hundred paintings, drawings, and sculptures.

In a *New York Times* article, Herbert Vogel explained: "We never bought anything because we thought it was important. We bought the things we liked. It's not about price. It's about feeling."

What, finally, was the monetary value of the Vogels' art collection when it was brought to the National Gallery, in Washington, D.C., in five moving vans? The museum's curator says that it's impossible to estimate the dollars-and-cents figure. But very few private collections make their way to institutions like the National Gallery unless the owners' name was something like Rockefeller or Getty.

The Vogels simply donated most of their collection to the museum, although some of it was purchased for what was surely a very substantial amount of money. Herbert and Dorothy Vogel plan to use the money to buy more art.

Referring to the Vogels' collection in the same *New York Times* article, Jack Cowart, curator of twentieth-century art at the National Gallery, acknowledged that the Vogels did it all for love, regardless of the price, even if it displaced them from their own apartment.[1]

The Five Fundamentals of Self-esteem

Regarding self-esteem, there are certain principles that you need to know.

Fundamental 1: You should be aware that self-esteem, or the lack of it, is at the root of all behavior, both positive and negative.

There simply is nothing more important than self-esteem in determining success or failure. As Jerry Lewis explained it in his film *The Nutty Professor*, "You'd better learn how to like yourself, because you're going to be spending a lot of time with you."

Fundamental 2: Remember that self-esteem is made up of both self-worth and self-trust.

Self-worth is simply the feeling of being glad that you're you, with your genes, your body, and your background. Self-trust is the functional belief in your own ability positively and effectively to control what happens to you in a world of uncertainty.

Fundamental 3: Realize that no opinion and no judgment is so vitally important to your own growth and development as that which you hold of yourself.

The most important conversations, briefings, meetings, and lectures you will ever have are those that you hold in the privacy of your own mind.

Fundamental 4: Remember that no eyes will ever critique a video of you, a photo of you, a reflection of you in a store window, or a full-length view of you in the mirror as you step out of the shower, as sharply and critically as your own eyes.

Make an effort to feel good about your physical self, including how you look, how you dress, and how you think. If you don't feel good about those things, take control and make the changes you need to make.

Fundamental 5: You can be your own worst enemy, or your own best friend.

Realize that, once and for all, *you* hold the key to your personal success and happiness.

The Voices of the Past

By accepting the five fundamentals of self-esteem we've just covered and by making them a part of how you look at the world, you'll be taking a big step toward harnessing the power of positive self-esteem, both in your work and in your personal life.

Corresponding to these five constructive ideas, however, there seem to be a common set of self-destructive beliefs that prevent most people from achieving their potential. Terry Orlick identifies these beliefs in a wonderful book called *In Pursuit of Excellence*. These destructive beliefs can be present even in the minds of world-class athletes and individuals with tremendous gifts in music, art, business, and all the professions. Do any of these Self-Destructive Beliefs sound familiar to you?[2]

FIVE SELF-DESTRUCTIVE BELIEFS

Self-destructive Belief 1: You must always prove yourself to be thoroughly competent, adequate, and achieving. You must perform as perfectly as possible in all situations.

Self-destructive Belief 2: You must always have the love and approval of the significant others in your life. You must always be right in their sight.

Self-destructive Belief 3: If you are afraid of something, if you are wrong about something, if you have made any kind of mistake, you must dwell on the problem. You have an *obligation to worry*.

Self-destructive Belief 4: You have little or no ability to change your feelings toward the things that happen to you, because they are caused by external pressures. You are a victim of life's circumstances.

Self-destructive Belief 5: You live with the child of your past, therefore you are compelled to behave, perform, and feel in a consistent manner for the rest of your life, because of that all-important influence.

Those are devastating negative beliefs, aren't they? But we all tend to let them creep into our lives much more than we should.

Well, what can be done about it?

In an address to the National Figure Skating Coaches in Vail, Colorado, Dr. Bruce Ogilvie spoke about what has most concerned him during his many years of offering mental training skills to individuals seeking peak performance. That concern centers on the desire of many athletes for some kind of quick fix or instant solution to the problems they encounter. This simply isn't feasible, according to Dr. Ogilvie, because permanent change must be preceded by considerable self-reflection. Real progress is only possible when the performer has an "Ah hah!" experience in which he or she accepts the rational cause behind the problem, and takes responsibility for its solution.

Referring to the mental enslavement of potential champions by their self-destructive beliefs, Dr. Ogilvie uses the phrase "voices of the past." Those voices can talk you into just about anything. Ogilvie instructs elite athletes to listen carefully to their own internal dialogue, in order to uncover anything that might prevent them from becoming all they can be.

If you've ever wondered about the scientific validity of the power and importance of your own self-talk, read Dr. Bruce Ogilvie's comments concerning the mind-set of Olympic-class figure skaters:

> We must honor the internal dialogue of the individual skater before we make suggestions about mental training strategies. It becomes critically important to discover how the athlete is mentally processing his or her experience as a skater. We speak of this as the athlete's cognitive style, internal dialogue or self-talk. Each performer has a private language, part conscious and part unconscious, which becomes the reference point from which his or her actions flow. There is no question that thought gives birth to action, for better or for worse."[3]

The "Unholy Trinity"

A prevalent form of self-talk sabotage that exists in both athletes and business professionals is what Dr. Ogilvie calls the "Unholy Trinity" of Denial, Rationalization, and Repression.[4]

Denial can negate the validity of a fine performance, or it can be an attempt to place the blame elsewhere after a disappointment. Have you ever been unable to accept the fact that you've actually closed a difficult sale, or made a successful presentation, or negotiated a well-deserved raise? Have you ever used phrases like, "It wasn't all that good," or "I was just lucky"? That's denial in action. On the other hand, when things are getting tense with your supervisors, does your self-talk say, "I don't have a problem! They have a problem!" That's the other side of denial.

Rationalization is a more philosophical form of denial. Instead of feeling angry, you resign yourself to the idea that things simply happened beyond your control. You may tell yourself you were too tired, or that you were too tense, or that the room was too small, or some other excuse. There are an infinite number of ways to transfer your own responsibility onto external circumstances.

The worst thing about rationalization is that it can be so convincing. A good rationalizer can talk everyone within earshot into just about anything.

In a business setting, rationalization can function almost like group hypnosis, and the first one to snap out of the trance can often create quite an impact. Years ago, for instance, in the early days of automobile travel, people were convinced that you couldn't drive in the winter. Around the middle of November they used to put their cars up on blocks until spring, and all the dealers would close down their businesses. But there was one small Ford dealer from the middle of South Dakota who kept sending orders to Detroit all through the winter months. Ford's sales manager finally made a trip out to South Dakota to see what was going on. He discovered that the dealer was a big, awkward young fellow who was so naïve and isolated that he'd never heard that you couldn't sell cars in the wintertime, so he just went ahead and sold them! Once the word got out to the other dealers that they'd better stop letting the weather dictate their closing hours, January became Ford's peak sales month.[5]

The last form of destructive self-talk is repression. Repression involves withholding your inner feelings about performance or behavior, even from yourself. This is perhaps the most dangerous member of the Unholy Trinity. Repressive self-talk says, "Disappointed? Who, me? I'm not disappointed. I really don't want to discuss the matter now. This isn't a good time for me. I'm tired and I've got a lot on my mind."

Ironically, it's often highly motivated individuals who slip into negative self-talk, simply because they're always trying too hard to do their best. In a word, they're perfectionists.

If you're determined to be perfect every time you're called upon, you're asking for trouble.

Perfectionism and Protectionism

Beneath those perfectionist strivings, frustration, anger, resentment, and even self-ridicule can easily take root.

Athletes bent upon perfection seem to resist the idea that the learning process for both mental and physical skills is a process of trial and error, with peaks, valleys, and plateaus of performance. Any failure on their part to live up to their impossibly high standards results in an inner tirade of negative self-talk. What's more, this self-talk serves only to sabotage their progress. A skater may have hit almost every requirement in a long routine, but barely missed hitting a perfect edge on one particular landing. Fixation on that single imperfection can needlessly destroy any sense of personal accomplishment.

Almost a century ago, Charles Schwab was paid the modern equivalent of twenty million dollars a year to run Andrew Carnegie's steel empire. This is how Schwab described his personal management style:

> I consider my ability to arouse enthusiasm to be the greatest asset I possess, and I believe the way to develop the best in anyone is by appreciation and encouragement. There is nothing else that kills ambition like criticism from superiors. So I never criticize anyone. I am anxious to praise but slow to find fault. If I like something, I am hearty in my appreciation and lavish in my praise.[6]

I think there's an important lesson in those words, and it's not just about how to talk to your employees. It's about how to talk *to yourself*. When you engage yourself in an internal dialogue, are you "hearty in your appreciation and lavish in your praise"?

If you're like many people, however talented, the answer may very well be "No."

Strongly achievement-oriented individuals often feel that humiliation and self-criticism are the only motivational forces that can generate enough energy to push them toward their personal and professional goals.

In a sense, it's as if they're afraid of jinxing themselves. They're trying to *protect* themselves from happiness!

These people feel compelled to deny themselves any joy or sense of accomplishment, because they're convinced even a little bit of satisfaction would somehow reduce their drive to win. The hug, the compliment, local and regional awards, top scores, and flowers of recognition can't be allowed to intrude upon the negative self-talk that dictates, *"I will never allow myself satisfaction in the absence of perfection."*

If you notice this tendency in yourself as you walk the fine line between self-sabotaging perfectionism and the healthy pursuit of excellence, here are some questions to keep in mind, inspired by the book *The Pursuit of Excellence* by my friend Ted Engstrom:

- Are you trying to do *your* best, or to be *the* best? Perfection struggles to reach impossible goals, while excellence enjoys meeting high standards within reach.

- Are you motivated by a desire for success, or a fear of failure? Perfection-seekers remember mistakes and dwell on them, while achievers of excellence correct mistakes and learn from them.

- Are you enjoying the process of success, or are you focused on the product, which must be perfect? Perfection values *what you do,* while excellence values *what you are.*[7]

Self-worth and Self-trust

Understanding the above questions is a good way to begin internalizing two components of self-esteem that I mentioned earlier—self-worth and self-trust.

You must believe that you are as worthy of happiness and success as anyone. You are worthy in your own way, regardless of how you may differ from others.

And you must learn self-trust, which is the ability to feel positive, responsible, and in control of what takes place as you try to test your limits.

A Triple-Axle Off the Merry-Go-Round

I can think of one Olympic champion who finally grabbed that gold ring and made it his own, but whose earlier life was a merry-go-round of pain and illness, of feeling unworthy and rejected under an impossible demand for perfection.

This sense of unworthiness began, perhaps, with a sense of his own physical limitations.

He had little evidence to believe that he controlled what happened to him. The very real test he faced each day was just staying alive.

When he was two years old, this adopted child of two college professors suddenly and inexplicably stopped growing, and his health started to fail. A team of doctors gave him six months to live. Finally, after several life-threatening emergencies, he was diagnosed correctly as suffering from Shwachman's syndrome, a rare disease that inhibits digestion of nutrients in food. Intravenous feedings of vitamins and supplements allowed him to regain his strength, but his growth was permanently stunted.

Confined to hospitals for long periods of time until the age of nine, he quietly plotted his revenge on the kids who taunted him and called him "peanut." He recalled many years later that subconsciously "the whole experience made me want to succeed at something athletic."

Sometimes his sister, Susan, went ice skating at the local rink, and he would go along to watch. There he stood, a frail, undergrown kid, with a feeding tube inserted through his nose and down into his stomach. When he wasn't using it, one end of the tube was taped behind his ear.

One day, as he watched his sister whirl around the ice, he turned to his parents and said, "You know, I think I'd like to try skating."

He tried it. He loved it. And he went at it with a passion.

Here was something fun at which he could excel, where height and weight weren't important. During his medical checkup the following year, the doctors were startled to discover that he had actually started growing again. It was too late for him to reach "normal" size, but neither he nor his family really cared. He was recovering and succeeding. And he had a goal.

The doctors believe that the combination of the cold ice rink and the intensity of his physical activity produced some almost magical, biochemical change in his body. *He* believes he skated his way out of his former condition and into a whole new world.

None of the kids taunt and tease him today. Instead, they all cheer and rush to get his autograph. He has just completed another dazzling performance on the world professional ice skating tour, with a long string of triple jumps, complicated maneuvers, and athletic moves, capped off with a racing front flip that brought him to a sudden stop inches from the audience.

At five feet three inches and 115 pounds of pure muscle and electrifying energy, former Olympic gold medal figure skating champion Scott Hamilton stands as tall and as proud as any winner. Scott's size did not limit his reach. Don't let doubts limit yours.

You must find the courage to enter your own arena and embrace the risk that every champion takes. You must accept the rewards and consequences of your own behavior.

This doesn't mean that you will close every sale or win every promotion. Scott Hamilton certainly didn't hit every triple-axle jump he ever attempted, especially during the initial learning phase. Success in developing any skill requires a basic trust in your ability that should never be allowed to waver. True confidence doesn't precede this trust, but is built upon it.

Ten Self-affirming Beliefs

Below are Ten Self-Affirming Beliefs you can incorporate into your life to help you bolster your self-acceptance and self-trust. You might want to photocopy them or write them down. I have them framed on my desk and I carry them inside my brief-case, so they're with me wherever I go. These inspirational ideas were inspired by observations made by Terry Orlick in his book, *In Pursuit of Excellence*.

1. I control my thoughts, emotions, and actions and I direct them to improve the quality of my health, my relationships, my work, and my life.
2. I am a good, valuable, and worthy person.
3. I am fully capable of achieving the goals that I set for myself today.
4. I trust my abilities and my judgment in taking risks that

will test my limits, and I am willing to live with the consequences and rewards of my decisions.

5. I am responsible for the values by which I live.

6. I learn from problems and setbacks, and through them, I can find opportunities for improvement and growth.

7. My spirit, mind, and body are a powerful team, which I set free to excel.

8. I am my own best friend and coach. When I talk to myself, I am encouraging, supportive, and respectful.

9. Every day I am becoming more knowledgeable, more aware, more curious, more caring, more adaptable, more successful, and more in control.

10. Regardless of what happens in my life, I have decided to be happy.[8]

CHAPTER FOUR

Fame, Fortune, and Integrity

The little old (rich) lady from Pasadena

Good news, bad news

Family business

Seven traits of a genuine leader

An American original

The Little Old (Rich) Lady from Pasadena

Rodeo Drive in Beverly Hills is where the rich and famous celebrities congregate to shop and be seen.

As the story goes, an attractive, well-dressed woman, probably in her late sixties but looking much younger, had spotted a parking place right in front of the Gucci store. She pulled up parallel to the Rolls in front and was ready to back into the open spot in her new white Mercedes sports coupe.

Before she could even turn the wheels, a young man driving a silver Corvette, with the top open and the stereo blasting, whipped right into her parking space.

She slammed on the brakes, got out of her car, and marched up to the other driver's window. She scolded him sternly: "You can't get away with that!"

The young man adjusted his Carrera sunglasses, smiled, and replied calmly: "Yes, I can, ma'am. I'm young and I'm quick!"

Whereupon the smartly dressed matron got in her car, shoved it in reverse, gunned the engine, and knocked his Corvette over the curb into the parking meter.

Stunned for a moment, the young man ran to her car and shouted: "Hey, you can't get away with that!"

The lady smiled and replied sweetly: "Oh, yes, I can, son. I'm old and I'm rich!" Then she peeled rubber and drove away.

I guess we all want to be rich, and live to be as old as possible, and do exactly what we want. That's perfectly natural. We'd all like to be able to trash (and be able to pay for) a dented-in Mercedes, a Corvette, and a parking meter just to prove a point. Of course, we all want to remain young and vital, too. Slick and quick, so to speak.

But isn't there also a desire for something beyond materialism? I think there is, and it's just as real as the wish to be able to wreck an expensive car or two. Just as there's a side of ourselves that longs for power and money, there is also a genuine desire to live each moment with integrity and principle.

Can these two sides of ourselves get along? Can they coexist and live together comfortably, or are they hopelessly incompatible? In this chapter, I will show you what it takes for a champion to maintain his or her integrity despite external pressures. And you will see what happens when strength of character fails.

A great deal is at stake. It seems as though greed and money, on the one hand, and honesty and integrity, on the other, are destined to compete for our individual and collective consciousness as we complete one century and enter a new one. The world is watching to see if ours is a nation of *shining* stars or of *shooting* stars.

The shooting stars have certainly been falling: Ivan Boesky, Pete Rose, Charles Keating, Michael Milken, and, by the time you read this, there will no doubt be many more. Names that once were destined for the Hall of Fame are hanging in the Hall of Shame.

Good News, Bad News

No nation has ever survived its own success indefinitely. That's the Bad News. Whenever a society got to the top of the league, it forgot to keep doing what it did to get on top in the first place, and down it came to take its place in the minor leagues.

The Good News is that there are signs that America may be able to turn it all around as we prepare to begin the twenty-first century. To stretch a metaphor, this may go down in history as the greatest national comeback season of all time.

The main reason for optimism is that we really do seem to understand that we've got to get our values in order. We're also beginning to realize that there's only one way to do that: *Total integrity in our personal and professional lives.*

People today, especially young people, need far fewer critics and far better role models. By setting an example of honesty, consistency, and commitment in all your relationships, you can create a kind of wealth for yourself and your family that's of much greater value than fame and fortune as we usually understand it.

By failing to set a positive example, you can invite serious trouble. For example, one of the most powerful and prevalent behavior-shaping influences in the world today isn't a human being, or even a cartoon character like Bart Simpson.

It's an *attitude*. I call it Silent Approval.

Silent Approval occurs when authority figures—whether they're heads of families or leaders of companies—look the other way when actions conflict with their stated principles. Silent Approval can also take the form of a negative example set by leaders, perhaps subconsciously, without anyone really being openly aware of the message that's being sent.

The mechanism is the same, whether it's at work or at home. Tell your kids to clean their rooms, and they'll check out the condition of your garage. Urge your employees to come early and stay late, and they'll be sure to notice just what time *your* car enters and leaves the parking lot.

Whatever you do *consistently*, whether good or bad, is what people are going to take as the truth. As Tom Peters states in his book *Thriving on Chaos: A Handbook for Management Revolution*, your true priorities as a leader are communicated by your handling of dozens of small issues. If you're pushing for quality control in your company but your plant's air conditioner is broken and your personal memos are full of typographical errors, you're not going to have a great deal of success. If you're demanding high grades from your kids in school but they never see you reading a book, they're going to learn from what you *do*, not from what you *say*.

Family Business

There are many similarities between running a business, coaching a team, and being the head of a family.

Spartan Motors, in Charlotte, Michigan, builds chassis for fire engines and other heavy-duty vehicles. In the last five years, the company's revenues have grown more than 500 percent, to almost ninety million dollars.

George Sztykiel runs Spartan Motors. Four times a year, he goes into the plant and personally reviews the organization's quarterly performance with each of the three shifts of workers. He always begins by asking recently hired workers to raise their hands.

Then he welcomes the new employees, and tells them that the company is run like a family, because, as he puts it, "That seems to be the most effective way people have discovered for getting along together."

At Spartan Motors, gains are shared by everybody in the form of quarterly bonuses. And when things are tough, everybody makes sacrifices.

There are no layoffs, ever. In 1976, workers took a 15 percent pay cut rather than see anyone let go.

In an interview, George Sztykiel explained why layoffs are unacceptable: "You wouldn't do that in your family, would you? If you have ten children and times get tough, you wouldn't send the three youngest ones out the door."[1]

Sztykiel himself is probably one of the lowest-paid CEOs in the American automotive industry, earning $78,000 a year. At the other end of the corporate spectrum, of course, you'll find the top three officers of Time Warner Inc., who earned $103.2 million, $14.7 million, and $11.3 million, including stock options.[2]

There's nothing shameful about making a lot of money as long as you're playing the game fairly. But it is interesting to note that Spartan Motors, with its low-paid executives, had a return on shareholder equity of 35 percent over the past five years. As George Sztykiel notes: "It would be easy for our competition to catch up to us. All they have to do is give up their big salaries and fancy offices."

Consistency is the opposite of Silent Approval, that concept I mentioned earlier. Spartan Motors is consistently spartan, in everything from the decor of the offices to the attitudes of the workers. I hope you can say the same about your organization's consistency and your role in it.

Seven Traits of a Genuine Leader

Here are seven specific things you can do to build consistency and integrity into your leadership style. I'm sure there are many more, but by putting these seven into practice in your daily life, you can be certain you're doing your best for your family and the people you work with.

1. Question your motives daily.

Before you make any decision, personal or professional, ask yourself: "Do I believe in what I'm doing here? Is this true, is this right, is this honest? If I do this, how will it affect the others involved?"

This is not only the best way to live in a moral sense, it's also eminently practical. It's the best way to ensure your success. In fact, to live according to any other standard is nothing short of self-destructive!

Lou Holtz has been a tremendously successful football coach for the University of Notre Dame, and the most remarkable thing about Holtz's teams is that they win in the classroom as well as on the football field. At Notre Dame, the bare minimum academic requirements set by the NCAA aren't good enough. Athletes have to take serious academic courses and they have to maintain at least a C average. Otherwise, they don't play. There are no special favors. If a player causes trouble or breaks the law, he's off the team, period.

Lou Holtz has three basic rules for his players: Do what's right; do your best; treat others as you want to be treated. Because if you don't, there will be a very tangible, self-destructive effect. You'll be creating a poor mental image of yourself, even if it's only subconsciously. And sooner or later, as a way to punish yourself, you'll find a way to undermine your own efforts.[3]

The result, of course, will be disaster for you and anyone who depends on you.

Psychologists have a term that describes the state of mind of an individual whose actions contradict his or her own principles of right and wrong. They call it *cognitive dissonance*.

Dissonance is a word that's often used to describe a certain type of atonal music. So, cognitive dissonance is a very apt term, because it suggests an orchestra that's trying to play two different compositions at once. When your actions are out of sync with your principles, you're making yourself the harried conductor of that very unfortunate orchestra. There simply is no possible way that the music is going to sound very good, least of all to you.

2. It's show, not tell.

Don't just tell your children, your peers, or your subordinates what to do. *Show* them by doing it yourself. How many of today's CEOs can personally build their company's product from the ground up? And when was the last time they ever actually did so?

3. Be your own investigative reporter.

At least once a week, imagine yourself as your own invisible investigative reporter. Pretend that, somehow, you were following yourself everywhere: at work, traveling, in your hotel room, in your home, tapping into your phone, and secretly opening your mail. What kind of story would you write? What kind of reading would it make? How do the areas of your life that only you know about compare with your "public self"?

Pete Rose was one of the most colorful and popular figures in baseball. He lived and breathed the game. By sheer effort and determination, he overcame his lack of great skills, and personified the general public's fantasy that anyone can come out of the sandlot and into the majors if he has passion and guts. In 1985, millions of fans watched in admiration as Pete Rose broke Ty Cobb's record of 4,191 major league base hits. Yet, Pete Rose's magnificent accomplishments all but vanished when the secret, self-destructive side of him was revealed.

His twenty-year career seemed to disappear before our eyes during the seventeen-month investigation of his alleged illegal activities. There was genuine confusion among the American public about how to treat this fallen hero. On one hand, the majority of people said it was right for Pete Rose to be sentenced to Federal prison for failing to report $350,000 in income. On the other hand, most people also believed he should be elected to the Baseball Hall of Fame.

There's no doubt that fame and fortune tend to breed arrogance and a sense of immense personal power. This can foster a sense of living beyond the laws that govern everyone else. Having power is like drinking salt water: The more you consume, the thirstier you get.

No matter how much wealth or recognition the world lays at your feet, don't allow your personal integrity to be contradicted by your behavior in any area of your life. It's not just a matter of preserving your reputation. It's a matter of living life with *character*. There is a lesson for all of us in the scandals of our public figures: You truly *cannot* separate your personal life from your professional life. You bring the same person to your place of business and home again. Integrity is nonsituational, and it is absolute.

4. Be loyal to your inner circle.

The two most sought-after traits of a top executive are honesty and loyalty. If you're looking for a real-life role model for these qualities, I'd like to nominate H. Ross Perot, the self-made billionaire about whom novelist Ken Follett wrote a best-selling book, *On Wings of Eagles*.

I had the privilege of observing, first-hand, the character-building years of Ross Perot, as a fellow midshipman with him at the United States Naval Academy at Annapolis, and during a summer cruise with him aboard the USS *Missouri*. More than any other person I've ever met, his principles are unswerving and uncompromised. He has total loyalty to his family, his friends, and his country.

At Electronic Data Systems, the company Ross Perot founded, every employee was treated as a brother and sister, no exceptions. Perot ate lunch in the cafeteria, usually traveled by commercial airline, and carried his own suitcases.[4]

Everyone also knew that Ross Perot would go to the ends of the earth to help them, whether it meant flying the wife of an associate to an eye specialist in an emergency or forming a team of private commandos to rescue two of his executives taken hostage in Iran.

I was surprised when he appeared to make a serious bid to become a presidential candidate in the past election, abruptly backed away, and then reentered the race. It seemed so out of character for him.

But most important, all the publicity, all the money, and all the power have not changed Ross Perot. He is never one to waste words. Perot says, "I see what's right, *and I do it.*"[5]

5. Follow through.

Talk is never enough, even when you're speaking the truth. When you promise something, do people believe it will really happen, or is there a question of whether you really mean it? Integrity implies an understanding that people can trust you to do what you say you'll do.

In short, promises should not be lightly given unless you want them lightly received.

6. Look up to those beneath you.

In 1958, an office worker in Boston was going through some old files. He discovered these rules of conduct for employees, issued in 1872.

- Office employees each day will fill lamps, trim wicks, and clean chimneys. Wash windows once a week.

- Each clerk will bring in a bucket of water and a scuttle of coal for the day's business.

- Male employees will be given an evening off each week

for courting purposes, or two evenings if they go regularly to church.

- Every employee should lay aside a sum of his earnings for the benefit of his declining years so that he will not become a burden to society.

- The employee who has performed his labor faithfully without fault for five years will be given an increase of five cents per day in wages, providing profits permit it.[6]

Of course, it's been a long time since employees were treated like this, but even now, too many managers look down on those they feel are beneath them. That kind of thinking is the enemy of leadership integrity.

David Ogilvy, founder of the giant advertising agency Ogilvy and Mather, used to give each new manager a Russian doll. The doll contained five progressively smaller dolls. A message inside the smallest one read: "If each of us hires people who are smaller than we are, we shall become a company of dwarfs. But if each of us hires people who are bigger then we are, Ogilvy and Mather will become a company of giants."[7]

Similarly, Masao Nemoto, as managing director of Toyota, wrote down his ten principles of management effectiveness and distributed them to his associates. Two of the principles dealt specifically with the relationship between a supervisor and his or her employees.

The first of these rules was, *Never punish for mistakes.* To most managers, this must seem like sheer insanity. Yet refusal to punish mistakes is the only way to be certain that errors will be reported immediately and in full, so that the root causes can be identified and amended. Assigning blame, especially in a large organization, only encourages people to cover things up.

The second rule was even more outrageous: *Managers must ask subordinates, "What can I do for you?"* At Toyota, meetings were routinely held in which supervisors asked subordinates whether anything could be done at the upper levels to make work more efficient or to improve the quality of the product. If requests were made, they were always acted upon immediately, lest anyone think that the meetings were just for show. Once the company leadership was seen as willing to help with problems, employees became more aggressive in attacking difficulties and in working to meet the organizational goals.[8]

7. Learn to watch your watch.

You may not have the artistic talent of a Michelangelo, or the musical ability of a Mozart. You may not have as much money as Warren Buffett has, or as much as Donald Trump *had*. But there's one thing that you have as much of as anyone else: time.

There are the same number of hours in your day as there were for Shakespeare or Einstein. Make the most of your time. Don't waste it, because when this minute is gone, it's gone forever.

How can you get the most out of your time? For starters, learn how to say "No." It's essential to cultivate an ability to politely refuse activities for which you have no time, no talent, or no real interest.

Conversely, don't be afraid to devote an extraordinary amount of time to a problem that requires a great deal of attention. When Vince Lombardi took over as coach of the Green Bay Packers, he chose Bart Starr to be his quarterback, despite the fact that Starr had demonstrated a weakness in throwing long passes. Lombardi had a theory that, once a weakness had been identified, hard work could turn it into a strength. He and Starr concentrated all their practice time on long passes until the quarterback had improved both his confidence and his physical ability. Bart Starr, of course, became one of the best all-around quarterbacks in the history of football.

An American Original

In 1985, *Forbes* magazine named Sam Walton the richest man in America. He disliked that label, but he didn't deny it. When he died seven years later, total market value of stock in Wal-Mart was worth twenty-three billion dollars.

How did Sam Walton build his empire? As he explained it, "High expectations are the key to everything."

In 1962, Sam Walton had high expectations. He wanted to open bigger Ben Franklin stores in rural areas. He already owned several Ben Franklin franchises, and he wanted to experiment with discount prices and lower profit margins. But company executives rejected his plan.

As a result, Sam Walton began to build his own organization. Eventually, it included hundreds of stores, thousands of trucks, and a fleet of planes—bought secondhand—to transport managers around the system. There were also rap songs and cheers to motivate employees, as well as college scholarships in the names of workers who made suggestions that improved service. As the price of Wal-Mart stock rose, employees benefited from pension plans and profit sharing. A cashier who retired in 1989 received $262,000 in benefits, according to Vance H. Trimble, author of Sam Walton's biography published by Dutton in 1990.

Through it all, Sam Walton led by example. By 4:30 in the morning, he was usually at his no-frills headquarters in Bentonville, Arkansas. On business trips, he often visited six Wal-Marts in a day. Often he flew his own twin-engine plane. He slept in budget motels or stayed at the homes of store managers. In recent years, he drove a red 1985 Ford pickup truck. Despite being slowed by cancer treatments, Sam Walton continued to visit dozens of stores each week and talked of lifting Wal-Mart's annual sales past one hundred billion dollars by the year 2000.

Less than a month before he died, Sam Walton was awarded the Presidential Medal of Freedom, the nation's highest civilian honor. He was described as "an American original, who embodies the entrepreneurial spirit and epitomizes the American dream."[9]

Remember: *High expectations are the key.* Demand integrity, respect for others, and hard work from yourself, because the values you live by are going to shape the future for you and those around you.

CHAPTER FIVE

Visualization of Victory

The mind is what matters
Seeing is believing, or is it?
A four-step plan for reducing stress
Letting your mind relax your body
"Going to the movies"
A visualization checklist

The Mind Is What Matters

His dream began as a preteen many years before, watching Olympic competition on television. Previews of coming attractions. In 1984, he had his chance. He was the top swimmer in the world in his event. He came to the Olympics in Los Angeles primed to win, and . . . finished second. The vision, the dream, was unfulfilled.

He went back to the dream, back into the pool, and started visualizing and training again. The vision was the gold medal in the 1988 Olympics in Seoul, Korea. But the dream went up in smoke at the Olympic trials. He didn't even make the team.

Like most people, he became discouraged. He put his dream for gold on hold, and went to law school at Cornell. For three years, he did very little swimming. But the vision burned inside. He couldn't extinguish the inner flame.

Less than a year before the 1992 Summer Games, he decided to go for it one last time. An old man in the youthful sport of swimming, he appeared to be jousting with windmills like a modern-day Don Quixote; even to consider the impossible dream of winning the 100-meter butterfly competition seemed foolish to most.

Emotionally, it was a sad and difficult period. His mother, Bianca, was dying of cancer. She would not be there to share the outcome of his quest. But she strengthened his resolve and dedication.

Surprisingly, he not only made the U.S. team, but won the qualifying race. His time, however, was more than a second slower than the world record. He would have to produce a miracle to be in contention.

More visualizing, more goals, more training. He planned the race in detail in his mind. It would last less than a minute, yet he saw it in crystal clear detail, from start to finish. He would get out fast, taking advantage of his speed. He would, he hoped, wear down his competitors and then outlast them to the finish.

Seeing the race in advance, he went out and swam it. Later that day, standing on the pedestal, watching the stars and stripes raised, listening to the national anthem, with the gold medal around his neck, Pablo Morales was transformed from visionary to victor. His dream had become reality.

When your eyes are open, you see the world that lies outside yourself. You see the items of the room you're in, the people, and the view of the landscape through the window. You take for granted that the objects are real and separate from yourself.

However, winners see the act of winning in advance—vivid, multidimensional, textured, clear. Champions know that "What you see, is who you'll be."

When you close your eyes, images and thoughts flow through your mind. You may review memories of past events, or preview future possibilities. You can daydream about what may be or what might have been, and your imagination will take you beyond the limits of space and time. Most people attach little importance to these inner visions. They may seem pleasantly irrelevant, or uncomfortably at odds with the accepted external reality.

If you're like most people, you grew up with the idea that "Seeing Is Believing." In other words, you need to physically see something with your own eyes to believe that it's real.

I know many successful people who live this way.

But there's a newer way of thinking that suggests, "*Before* you can see it, you have to *believe* it," which is the subject of a great deal of work by my friend and colleague Dr. Wayne Dyer. This premise holds that our belief system is so powerful that thoughts can actually cause things to happen in the physical world.

I also know many successful individuals who live according to this notion of reality.

So which concept is nearer the truth? Do you have to see it before you believe it, or believe before you see it?

The answer is, both are basically true. If you can see something in your mind's eye, and you imagine it over and over again, you will begin to believe it is really there in substance. As a result, your actions, both physical and mental, will move to bring about in reality the image you are visualizing.

It's important that you understand these ideas and take them to heart. They're fundamental to applying *The New Dynamics of Winning* in your professional and personal life, and to gaining the mind-set of a champion.

Seeing Is Believing, or Is It?

Let's focus for a moment on the real meaning of the phrase, *Seeing is believing*.

Today, neuroscience is demonstrating that even sights and

sounds below the level of conscious perception can have a powerful influence on behavior. In experiments conducted by Dr. Howard Shevrin, of the University of Michigan Medical Center, a word like *fear* was flashed on a screen for a thousandth of a second. As a result, electrodes on the subject's head, which registered electrical activity at the surface of the brain, transmitted a measurable response to the subliminal flashing of *fear*. Yet the subject was not aware that he'd seen the word. If asked, he would swear that he *hadn't* seen it. But in his "mind's eye," he did see it and responded accordingly.[1]

When I was at Annapolis, I underwent training in aircraft recognition. All of us midshipmen sat at one end of a hall while silhouettes of American and foreign military aircraft were flashed on a screen in rapid succession. We were supposed to write down the numerical designation and name of the planes, such as F-8U Crusader, MIG-21, A4D Skyhawk, and so forth. But the task became more difficult each week, because they kept adding more planes, scrambling the order, and speeding up the slide projector.

Finally, it got ridiculous, because the slides were going by so fast half of us only saw a blur, and some didn't see anything. I began to see planes that weren't even invented yet. When it came time for the final exam, I didn't know for certain *which* planes I was seeing. I wrote down hunches, intuitions, and reflex responses.

But when the test results were announced, virtually everyone had scored a perfect 100 percent. We *had* seen the planes, even if we didn't necessarily believe it. For me, that test proved that images can be stored and retained, unconsciously, at incredible speeds. And those stored images, when recalled, can enhance performance.

What about the thousands of flickering images we see on a TV screen? What about commercials? Do we have to *believe* the products really do all those amazing things before we buy them? Do viewers have to think that violent scenes in movies and TV are actually occurring in real life for there to be a negative effect on their behavior? Many people believe that violent fantasy has no impact on their lives whatsoever, because they think they're too intelligent to be swayed by it.

Well, I've got news for them. Whatever you see or experience, real or imagined, consciously or subliminally, when repeated vividly over and over, *does* affect your behavior, and definitely can influence you to buy a product or buy into a lifestyle, good or bad. Your beliefs are, quite simply, a function of what you see day in and day out. Information can be taken in almost unnoticed. You won't react to it until later, and you still won't be aware of what lies behind your response. In other words, what you see really is what you get, regardless of whether you know it or not.

You don't need to be watching slides of airplanes, or TV shows, or music videos, or commercials. You can be just lying down, or commuting to work, or walking through a park, and by seeing from within, in your mind's eye, you can change your life.

By rehashing fears and problems you can make yourself depressed. As a result, you can blow a sale, hurt a relationship, or lower your performance. By forecasting a gloomy outcome in your mind's eye, you can act as your own witch doctor and practice a modern-day kind of voodoo that will fulfill your negative prediction with uncanny accuracy.

On the other hand, by replaying in your mind's eye the best game you ever played, you can repeat that best game again, when the stakes are even higher and the pressure is on. And by mentally preplaying the best game you've ever *imagined,* you can set the stage for a world-class performance. This "instant replay" and "instant preplay" applies to anything from a successful sales call to the effective motivation of your employees or your children.

A Four-Step Plan for Reducing Stress

When Dr. Jerry May and I served as cochairmen of psychology on the U.S. Olympic Committee's Sports Medicine Council, we conducted a Sports Psychology Congress in conjunction with the last Olympiad held here in America. Some of the world's leading experts shared their insights on all aspects of mental training, including guided imagery and visualization techniques.

Dr. May told of a fifteen-year-old figure skater who kept falling down on the ice. She began visualization training. Before the end of her stay at the Olympic training center, she was able to relax and mentally picture herself successfully completing a difficult jump that she had previously been unable to perform. Within weeks of her return home, she telephoned her parents with the good news that she had not only completed the double axle in her mind, but on the ice as well!

Dr. Barbara Kolonay, a sports psychologist who was interviewing us for ABC, told of her use of mental rehearsal during basketball free-throw shooting at New York's Hunter College. The players were monitored by electromyographs, which are instruments used to measure muscle activity. As they sat in a deeply relaxed state shooting free throws in their imaginations, the electromyograms clearly illustrated that the athletes' muscles actually fired and performed in the exact sequence and motion, as if they were really standing at the foul line and shooting the ball through the basket. During visualization exercises, the mind can't tell the difference between a real performance and one that is imagined. And neither can the body.

So even if you don't believe that you're a champion just yet, and even if you don't believe that visualization techniques really work, I'll be willing to bet you that if you are open and receptive to the idea that you have been holding yourself back, and will honestly try to internalize the ideas in this program, you'll make progress that will be obvious to you and everyone close to you.

Before you can use your imagination effectively, you need to relax your mind and your body. Mental relaxation allows the right hemisphere of your brain more freedom because the verbal, judgmental, and analytical left hemisphere is quieted. Physical relaxation puts you in touch with your body's internal environment, without distraction. Unfortunately, if you're like many achievement-oriented individuals, relaxation may not come naturally, since the pressures of life in the corporate fast lane can equal anything faced by world-class athletes.

So, where to begin? Let's look first at some ways to reduce stress and foster mental relaxation.

In a course at Stanford University on creativity for business managers, instructors Michael Ray and Rochelle Myers have created a four-step method for identifying and defusing the tensions associated with business leadership.[2]

Step 1: Make a written list of all the issues that are causing you to feel stress.

The list should be as complete as possible, and should include personal as well as work-related factors. If you're behind on a deadline, and your car needs a new starter motor at the same time, both those items should be part of your list. The purpose of the list is to make yourself consciously aware of everything that's causing you to feel pressured, so that you don't fall prey to any unconscious, possibly self-defeating, reactions. The list should be updated regularly and, needless to say, it should be "for your eyes only."

Step 2: Read through your list.

Identify the items over which you have direct control, and which you can eliminate by a clearly defined action or sequence of actions. Then make a sublist of these avoidable stresses, together with the corrective actions you intend to take and *the specific time you intend to take them.* As soon as you've followed through on one of your solutions, cross off the appropriate item.

Step 3: Create a sublist

Many of the items on your stress list will probably be characterized by *uncertainty*. You aren't really sure to what extent the problem is under your control, or someone else's, or whether it's controllable by anybody at all. Write out a sublist of these poorly defined stressors. Beside each item, indicate an action you can take toward clarifying the problem and bringing it under control. For example, if you're worried about how the performance of another department may reflect on you, further investigation may reveal that your concern is unfounded, or you may find there's simply no way you can influence that area of the organization. In either case, once you've replaced uncertainty with fact, you'll have a better idea of how to proceed.

Step 4: Make the best of it!

After you've completed the two sublists described above, the problems that remain on your original inventory should be those which are clearly beyond your control. Sadly, in today's world there may be quite a few such items. The prime rate of interest, gloomy weather, root canal, and so forth, are simply *there,* whether you like it or not. Since these facts of life can't be altered, change for the better must take place *in you,* and in your ability to accept the unavoidable and make the best of it. If you're stuck in a traffic jam on the way to a meeting, pounding on the steering wheel will just make you feel worse. Instead, try thinking about other times your schedule was disrupted. Reassure yourself that the world didn't end on those occasions, and recognize that it won't end now either. Someday you'll be able to laugh about the situation you're in. So why not start now?

Letting Your Mind Relax Your Body

Dr. Thomas Tutko, cofounder of the Institute of Athletic Motivation, is one of the most respected sports psychologists in the country. For more than twenty-five years, Dr. Tutko has worked with medal-winning Olympians, as well as with outstanding professional athletes. He's the author of the book and audio program *Sports Psyching,* as well as several other popular works, including *The Psychology of Coaching.* Dr. Tutko has perfected relaxation techniques for the peak performers, and I'd like to share some of his research with you.

At the world-class level of athletic performance, there are three widely used methods of physical relaxation: Deep Breathing Exercises, Progressive Relaxation Exercises, and Autogenic Relaxation Exercises.

Deep Breathing

You breathe some twenty thousand times per day, or about fourteen times per minute, tensing and relaxing certain muscles with each breath. When you're nervous or fearful, your chest, throat, and diaphragm constrict, and your breathing becomes rapid and shallow. You need more air when you're under pressure, yet it's then that your breathing becomes inhibited. That's where the term "choking under pressure" comes from.

To combat the "choking" response, Dr. Tutko has developed the following deep-breathing exercise. It can be learned quickly, and requires only five or ten minutes to complete.

When you're doing this exercise for the first time, lie flat on your back on a bed or on the floor, with a pillow under your head. After a few sessions, you'll be able to perform the exercise while sitting, standing, or driving.

As you lie on your back, inhale slowly and deeply through your nose, filling your chest with air. Silently count from one to four, while imagining your chest filling slowly and completely with air.

Then, when you've inhaled fully, hold your breath for another four seconds. It should be just a comfortable pause. Finally, exhale through your mouth, slowly and without blowing. As you slowly and quietly let the air out through your mouth, think to yourself, "Easy, easy, easy."

Remember the three steps: Inhale deeply and completely through the nose. Hold it for a count of four, not enough time to feel any discomfort. Then slowly and quietly exhale through your mouth. After you've done this a number of times, you won't need to count anymore. Your breathing rate will naturally become slower.

According to Dr. Tutko, you can enhance the benefits of the exercise by giving yourself some positive suggestions.

For example, you might think to yourself, *Good feelings are coming into me as I inhale, and as I exhale all tension is leaving me. Whenever I'm under pressure I will be able to recall this exercise by taking a few deep breaths and repeating the words "Easy, easy, easy." These relaxing, positive feelings will automatically return to me.*

Progressive Relaxation

Progressive Relaxation was developed by Professor Edmund Jacobsen of Harvard University. The exercise takes roughly fifteen minutes, and can be done lying down or sitting in a straight-backed chair. It consists of tensing and relaxing the various muscle groups, for periods of five to ten seconds. You don't need to pay close attention to the timing of this exercise. Instead, focus all your attention on the feelings you experience.

Begin by tensing your dominant hand. Clench it into a fist, feel the tension for a few seconds, then release it and notice the contrasting feeling of relaxation. Repeat the procedure with the same hand.

Now tense the other hand into a fist, and then relax. Do it again.

Next, tense one arm so that the biceps is flexed, and then relax. Repeat, maintaining the tension just a second or two longer. Do the same with your other arm.

Tense your forehead. Then relax and repeat.

Clench your jaws tight. Relax and repeat.

Shrug and tense your shoulders.

Tighten your stomach muscles.

Tense your toes by pointing them downward. Then relax and repeat.

As you go through these sequences, try to concentrate on your sensations as intensely as you can. When you've tightened an individual muscle group, think *Let go* at the instant you relax. Try to become completely limp in one area after the other, and feel the tension drain away.

After you practice the progressive relaxation exercises for a week or two, you should be able to automatically relax your muscles simply by thinking the words *Let go*. Similarly, the words *Easy, easy, easy* should enable you to trigger the relaxed sensations of the deep-breathing exercise.

Autogenic Training

The use of words to help induce a state of physical relaxation is called Autogenic Training, which was first developed by a German psychiatrist named Johannes Schultz. It's been employed with great success by many Russian and Eastern European elite athletes. This technique also raises your sensitivity to visualization and verbal suggestion.

First, find a quiet place where there will be no noise or interruptions. The exercise takes about twenty minutes. You should either be lying flat on your back or sitting comfortably, with your eyes closed.

There are six autogenic exercises. Memorize the statements

that induce each desired state, and repeat them softly in your mind as you're going through each sequence.

The **First Autogenic Exercise** focuses on the concept of *heaviness*. Start with the right arm if you are right-handed.

Tell yourself: "My right arm is heavy."

Now repeat this statement at least six times, interspersing the words, "I'm relaxing and I'm at peace." For example: "My right arm is heavy. I'm relaxing. My right arm is heavy. I'm at peace." As you say the words to yourself you'll be learning how to release the tension in your arm to create a sensation of heaviness.

Next, move to your other arm and silently repeat the self-suggestion to yourself six times: "My left arm is heavy." Then, "Both of my arms are heavy." Repeat this six times.

Move to your right leg and then your left leg. Repeat the statements as before. Then concentrate on both legs: "Both of my legs are heavy. I'm relaxing. Both of my legs are heavy. I'm at peace."

Finally, tell yourself, "My arms and legs are heavy," and repeat this six times.

The **Second Autogenic Exercise** focuses on both *heaviness and warmth*. In addition to relaxing the muscles, this will also help you dilate your arteries.

Begin with the self-statement: "My right arm is heavy and warm." As before, repeat this six times.

Next, "My left arm is heavy and warm," six times. Then: "My right leg is heavy and warm. My left leg is heavy and warm."

The final key sentence for this exercise is: "Both of my arms and legs are heavy and warm."

The **Third Autogenic Exercise** focuses on the *heart rate*. Even during the compulsory figures competition, some Olympic ice skaters have heart rates as low as sixty beats per minute. This state of ultimate preparedness and calm wasn't inborn. They learned it.

Here the key self-suggestion is: "My heartbeat is slow and

regular.'' This is repeated six times, with the focus on actually feeling the heartbeat slow down to a steady, relaxed rhythm.

The **Fourth Autogenic Exercise** focuses on *respiration,* and on allowing the body to breathe by itself. Repeat silently: ''My breathing is relaxed and effortless.''

Creating *warmth in the abdominal area* is the purpose of the **Fifth Autogenic Exercise**. The phrase to repeat is: ''My stomach is warm.'' As you progress, you should become aware of a warming sensation in your abdominal area.

The final, **Sixth Autogenic Exercise** concentrates on *cooling the forehead.* Most tension-related headaches occur when constricted blood vessels suddenly open after being pressured. The increased rush of blood to the forehead through the dilated arteries causes pain. By cooling the forehead and warming your hands, feet, and abdominal area, you can prevent the onset of a headache or minimize its effects after it has begun. The key phrase for this last exercise is: ''My forehead is cool.'' Repeat it six times.

I highly recommend tape-recording the six autogenic training exercises in your own voice. Say each phrase slowly and softly, pausing for about two seconds between each one. Many people find it helpful also to play slow, soothing music in the background.

After four to six weeks of daily practice, you should be able to create the desired autogenic responses in just a few minutes, even without repeating the self-statements to yourself or listening to them on tape. All you'll need to do is sit quietly and remember the phrases and feelings from the practice sessions.

"Going to the Movies"

Now let's move on to visualization. To sports psychologists, this is known as Visual Motor Behavior Rehearsal, or VMBR.

As we discussed earlier, the mind cannot tell the difference between a real experience and one that has been vividly and repeatedly imagined. The brain accepts and reacts *automatically* to the information it receives in the form of pictures, sounds, or feelings. Some individuals respond better to one type of stimulus than to another. But no matter which you seem most attuned to, everyone can benefit greatly from enhancing his or her visual rehearsal capabilities.

There are two basic types of VMBR: receptive and programmed.

Receptive visualization is used to help answer a question or to find a solution to a problem. To begin, think consciously about the problem and try to understand it as best you can.

Now, close your eyes and imagine a blank white screen. Let the answer you're seeking appear gradually, in its own time. This technique can be especially helpful in recalling information that seems to be lost or forgotten.

Programmed VMBR is the better-known type of visualization technique. It involves creating and repeating a mental image of yourself performing a task successfully.

Jack Nicklaus, perhaps the greatest golfer of all time, is a firm believer in programmed visualization. He calls it "going to the movies." Nicklaus says he never hits a ball, even in practice, without first seeing each part of the shot in his mind's eye.

Interestingly, Nicklaus's mental movie camera runs backward. He begins by visualizing the final result of the shot. He imagines exactly how and where the ball will land, seeing the perfect outcome in exquisite detail.

The scene changes.

Now he visualizes how the ball gets to that ideal spot. Is it drawing or fading? How high is it flying? What does it do when it lands?

Then, one final scene. Nicklaus mentally sees the swing he needs to achieve this perfect shot. He imagines his setup, backswing, follow-through, and all the other things he must do to make exactly the shot he wants. Only after visualizing this entire sequence does he actually select his club and hit the ball. The entire process requires only a few seconds.

Of course, Jack Nicklaus isn't perfect. He doesn't always make the shot he imagines. But he's made it more than almost anyone who's ever played the game.

Stephen King, the best-selling novelist, has a personal visualization technique, too.[2] In a magazine interview, King said, "I've never felt like I was actually creating anything. For me, writing is like walking through a desert. All at once, poking up through the ground, I see the top of a chimney. I know there's a house under there, and I'm pretty sure that I can dig it up if I want. It's like the stories are already there. That's how I feel."

A Visualization Checklist

Here are some specific tips for visualizing successfully:

1. When you visualize yourself doing something, make it an *action scene* in which there's *movement*.

This is Visual Motor Behavior Rehearsal, and the object is to create a neurological pathway enabling your muscles to "remember" the sequence of movements that make up an action. Therefore, no still pictures please.

2. Visualize *both* the successful outcome and the steps leading up to it.

Olympic athletes mentally run through what they want to do and how they want to do it well before they arrive at the arena. They imagine the sights, sounds, temperatures, spectators, and the other competitors—and then they focus on their own performances. Some even include a clock or stopwatch in their imagery to ensure that the timing and pacing in their minds are exact.

You can do similar visualizations for meetings, sales calls, or, in my case, weddings! How would you like to have four daughters all reaching marriageable age at almost the same time? My wife visualizes every minute in detail in advance. I visualize myself with a giant checkbook on my back!

3. Visualize conditions and things that are *consistent with your principles and moral values.*

If there's a conflict, you'll be less likely to get your mind and body working in concert. Ask yourself if what you are picturing is really in your own best interest and in the best interest of those who will be affected.

4. Most important, when you visualize yourself, see yourself in the present, *as if you are already accomplishing your goal.*

Make certain your visual image is as you would see it through your own eyes, not watching through the eyes of a spectator. If you're a skier, your imagery would appear in your mind as if an invisible TV camera were mounted on your shoulder looking exactly where your eyes are focused during a ski run, and feeling the same sensations. If you need to give a speech, you should imagine exactly how the audience will look sitting in front of you.

To strengthen your visualization capability, start making mental notes on all the experiences that make up your life. Take in as many sights, sounds, smells, textures, and tastes as you can. Recreate in your mind the beauty of a sunrise or sunset. Feel the wet sand of a beach between your toes. As you become more curious, observant, and in tune with your surroundings, you'll find your powers of visualization improving greatly. And the more often you see the winner's circle in your mind's eye, the sooner you'll arrive there in person.

CHAPTER SIX

Self-confidence and Self-transformation

Becoming one with the bull's-eye
How to get out of your own way
Blocking out the blocks
Self-statements: movies where you're the star
The three types of self-talk
The power of self-transformation

Becoming One with the Bull's-eye

A world-champion archer raises his bow, his eyes locked on the center of the target thirty yards away. At this moment, he doesn't want to see, hear, or feel anything except the center of the bull's-eye. With his bow drawn taut and his eyes on the target, he takes a quick, silent scan of his body and his mind. If something feels even slightly wrong, he'll lower the bow, relax, and draw again. If all systems check out, he holds his focus steady and simply lets the arrow fly, confident that it will find the mark.

Is this condition of calm confidence reserved exclusively for sports superstars? Well, it may be easiest to recognize in world-class athletes, but it's really a state of being we've all known. You've probably experienced it more often than you realize.

To understand fully how each of us can get in the peak

performance zone in our own careers and personal lives, you can use the analogy of the archer. In a sense, we are all archers trying to hit our personal bull's-eyes on the first try. Once we have trained our muscles and nervous system to shoot an arrow into the middle of a target, why can't we put it into the center every time?

I once drove a golf ball straight down the fairway nearly three hundred yards. It not only felt great, but it amazed me and the rest of my foursome, because most of my drives enjoy an excursion in the woods, a cool dip in the lake, or a trip to the beach in the sandtrap. Why can't I repeat that three-hundred-yard, arrow-straight drive whenever I want?

Or can I?

Actually, there's a great deal you can do toward consistently achieving peak performance. You can start by learning to detect and eliminate self-sabotaging thoughts, feelings, and habits. Then, by using the same positive mental techniques that work for an archery champion or a professional golfer, you can sell more policies, program more software, service more clients, or meet whatever challenges *you* face every day.

How to Get Out of Your Own Way

It's mysterious, isn't it? One individual faces challenge and adversity and becomes negative, frustrated, and pessimistic. Everywhere he looks, externally and internally, he finds reasons why he can't succeed. Instead of fixing his mind on what he wants, he fixes on blame, and fears what is going to happen.

Another person faces the same type of pressure situation and becomes stronger, more focused, and determined. His performance becomes increasingly more inspired and effective. In spite of the environment around him, he continues to move forward and, in the process, becomes an inspiration to everyone.

Why does one competitor cave in under the pressure and the other seem to thrive on it?

There are two great misconceptions about peak performance. The sooner you stop believing them, the better off you'll be.

First, there's the idea that *you must always bear down and try your hardest to win.*

This surfaces all too often in school sports, with coaches or parents yelling, "Come on! Get mad! The championship is at stake!" Or the phrasing can be negative, which is even worse: "Don't quit! Don't choke! Whatever you do, don't lose!"

In the business world, this misconception expresses itself through threats, deadlines, "bottom-line thinking," and all manner of pressures exerted by managers on employees, and by employees on themselves. Obviously, things have to get done on time, and if a company hopes to stay in business, a profit has to be made. The test of an effective manager, however, is his or her ability to communicate these requirements as potential *opportunities* rather than potential *catastrophes.* It's that simple.

The second self-defeating misconception is almost a mirror image of the first.

Now, instead of trying to clench your fists, grit your teeth, and bear down, you convince yourself that you shouldn't think about *anything*—that your mind should just be a blank screen and everything you do should be spontaneous.

The fact is, many people mistake spontaneity for something it's not. True spontaneity is learned behavior. When high-performing individuals appear to be acting effortlessly—to be "on a roll"—it's really because of all the training that's come earlier. During an actual performance, champions are simply pushing the playback button to access their physical and mental preparation. That's something very different from putting your mind in the freezer and your emotions in cold storage.

During her many years as an international tennis star, Chris Evert always seemed to grow more relaxed as the intensity of competition increased. She won eighteen Grand Slam titles— including the U.S. Open six times, the French Open seven times, and Wimbledon three times. I remember watching her at the U.S. Open in New York back in 1971, in a match against Mary Ann Eisel. Six different times, Chris was one point away from losing the match. Each time she came back to win the point, and finally she won the match.

In the tennis gallery, you could literally see it happening. Chris would slap her leg. That was a trigger for her to collect her thoughts.

She would take a deep breath, narrow her eyes, and focus totally on one moment in time. You could actually see her blocking out every sound and distraction in the stadium, moving inward, locking her mind on the task at hand.

Champions in all walks of life learn to achieve this relaxed focus. It's very different from lack of intensity. Rather, it's centering attention only on what's important for flawless execution. External thoughts and unwanted tensions are erased. Everything is on target.

Blocking Out the Blocks

In addition to the two major misconceptions mentioned above, there are a number of specific mental blocks that can get in the way of peak performance. You should be aware of them, and routinely audit yourself to see if they're causing you to fall short of your full potential. By asking yourself the following questions before you embark on a significant undertaking, you can increase dramatically your chances of success.

Question 1: Are you feeling optimistic?

In my years of research on human achievement and accomplishment, one of the most striking things I've learned is that a high expectation of success is the single most valuable quality you can bring into any challenging situation.

A high expectation of success is more important than natural ability or the lack thereof. It's more important than practice or preparation. This has been proven in any number of controlled experiments.

When experimental subjects are told that a given task they're being asked to perform is very easy, their performance invariably turns out to be much better than an equal number of subjects who are led to believe the task will be extremely difficult. This is true whether it involves an athletic contest, an IQ test, or any combination of physical and intellectual challenges.

Therefore: Don't just hope for the best, learn to *expect* the best, even if you have to force yourself to do so.

Remember, too, that optimism is contagious.

In any collective enterprise, your own optimism will rub off on the other members of the group and increase the probability of your organization's success. This doesn't mean that you should walk around with a silly grin on your face. It does mean that you should see the glass as half full instead of half empty, and even if you still *see* it as half empty, *say* it's half full!

Question 2: Are you drowning in a sea of adrenaline?

There's no doubt that it's good to feel optimistic and keyed up, as long as this leads to a performance that's energetic and free-flowing. But don't let yourself get too "high"—because if something goes wrong, your overload of enthusiasm can change into a dangerous excess of gloom and doom.

When the legendary oil man H. L. Hunt recalled building his fortune as a wildcatter, he said that one of the most important lessons he learned was to "always be prepared for sudden change." No, he wasn't talking about finding dimes on the sidewalk. He meant that you should never let yourself get so wrapped up in an idea, a plan, or a project that you lose the ability to retain your balance if the whole thing falls through. That's good advice.

Question 3: Are you replaying yesterday's mistakes?

Worrying about past errors or failures surely qualifies as one of the most self-destructive pastimes you can possibly inflict upon yourself. What happened earlier has absolutely no influence on what happens today unless you choose to let it. Let me emphasize the word *choose,* because you are in total control here, whether you think so or not.

President Calvin Coolidge is remembered mainly as a man who didn't waste words. But he waxed uncharacteristically eloquent on the importance of giving your best effort right now regardless of what happened yesterday:

> Nothing in the world can take the place of determination. Talent will not; nothing is more common than unsuccessful men with talent, and unrewarded genius is almost a proverb. Education will not; the world is full of educated derelicts. Persistence and determination alone are omnipotent. The slogan "Press On" has solved and always will solve the problems of the human race.[1]

Question 4: Are you confident of your preparation?

There's a dream that many people have had. I've certainly had it many times. Freud knew about it and called it the Examination Dream.

The dream can have many variations, but it basically consists of finding yourself faced with a written examination and being totally helpless to answer even a single question. I suppose "dream" is really the wrong word for this. It most definitely qualifies as a nightmare!

This dream can have its counterpart in reality whenever you go into a situation less than thoroughly prepared. Conversely, the certain knowledge that you're well trained and "ready for anything" is one of the best ways to assure success.

In his best-selling book *Swim With the Sharks Without Being Eaten Alive,* Harvey Mackay describes how marketers in his company are required to fill out a sixty-six-item questionnaire about prospective customers before making the initial sales call. Later, the questionnaire is continually updated with information ranging from the customer's favorite sports to the most recent quarterly earnings of his company. Armed with this much information, Mackay's salespeople are able to walk into a prospect's office with total confidence that they're well prepared and that nothing is going to take them by surprise.

Question 5. What about the A.N.T.s?

Ants can ruin a picnic, and A.N.T.s can ruin just about anything! A.N.T.s is an acronym for Abstract Negative Thoughts, and their presence is one of the surest signs that you're not ready to perform at your best.

Let's take a look at some A.N.T.s in action. Suppose you're demonstrating a new product to executives at a big manufacturing company. As you park your car and walk toward the company's headquarters, you're feeling apprehensive.

Then, as if by magic, thoughts start creeping into your mind: "Is my product really any good?" "Am I the right kind of person to be doing this kind of work?" "If this meeting goes badly, will it actually make any difference in the great scheme of things?" "Can the world really go on much longer?"

Notice that there's a dual pattern to these thoughts. They become increasingly abstract, and increasingly negative. What they're really doing is *distancing* you from the challenge you're facing.

In a cop-out sort of way, they're an attempt to deal with the worry you're feeling. You're trying to tell yourself not to feel anxious because you never really had a chance anyway, and, besides, what difference does it all make?

With this type of thinking, you'll be pondering the existence of life in other galaxies by the time you finish walking across the parking lot.

To defeat abstract negative thinking, you must first recognize that it's an extremely common, almost reflexive response to stressful situations. Acknowledge it, but don't buy into it.

Champions are disciplined thinkers. They recognize the relationship between what they think and how much pressure they experience during competition. They know that when people feel stress, it's something that they're doing to themselves. And, unfortunately, for most people it's an unconscious and automatic process, like a computer reading its program.

To avoid this kind of self-sabotage, train yourself to focus on the concrete, tangible, and *positive* aspects of what you're about to do. Think of some physical action or gesture that will snap yourself out of an A.N.T. trance and bring you back to reality.

As I mentioned, Chris Evert used to slap her leg. Even if you have to hit yourself over the head, do whatever it takes to get your mind on the here and now.

Question 6: Are you thinking too much about the outcome, and not enough about the process?

When you're truly in the peak performance zone, there's a natural flow of energy between mind and body. You're not looking at the scoreboard, whether that means the number of dollars in your paycheck or the number of strokes in your handicap. You're not trying to win. Instead, winning seems effortless and expected.

The process is its own reward. *It's fun.*

In professional sports, where millions of dollars are spent on individual athletes, teams are eager to do everything possible to protect their investments. Contracts routinely prohibit players from risking injury in off-season recreational activities, and even touch football or pick-up basketball games are forbidden. Yet, Michael Jordan, arguably the greatest basketball player of all time, insisted on a so-called "love of the game" clause in his contract which allows him to participate in informal, playground competitions whenever he wants.

Think of it! Michael Jordan has been playing basketball virtually all his life. He plays almost a hundred games a year at the most intense level of professional competition. He earns millions of dollars for his efforts, and he still wants to be able to go out and play basketball *for the love of the game*. No wonder he's a winner.

Self-statements: Movies Where You're the Star

What you've just been reading are some of the things you should watch out for when you're called upon to perform at the championship level. Now that we've looked at the negatives, let's consider the many positive things you can do to bring out the best in yourself.

In our discussion of visualization, I mentioned the awesome power of self-suggestion. I'd like to return to that subject, because the implications are enormous. You not only have the ability to replay past experiences as if they were happening again, you also have the ability to create, in effect, a personal preview of coming attractions in your own mind. You can literally preplay the future.

Since the mind can't distinguish between a real experience and one that is repeatedly and vividly imagined, you can be the scriptwriter, main character, and director of a triumphant life story like *Chariots of Fire*. Of course, you can also choose a laborious soap opera like *General Hospital*.

It all depends on the kinds of messages you give yourself every day.

Make no mistake: You are your own most important judge. There is no opinion as important to your performance and well-being as the opinion you have of yourself. The most important meetings, briefings, coaching sessions, and conversations you'll ever have are the conversations you have with yourself.

In the world of the Olympic and professional athlete, this language of the mind is referred to as the *self-statement*. By creating these powerful verbal, visual, and emotional "scripts," you can evoke a more healthy and desired response in yourself. Through your self-statements, you can help elevate your performance level in an especially challenging situation. The following information on self-talk is derived from information compiled by the U.S. Olympic Committee Sports Medicine Council.

The Three Types of Self-talk

General self-talk applies to those affirmative statements about yourself that can be used at any time and place for a feeling of general well-being and confidence. Some examples are: "I like myself"; "I'm glad I'm me"; "I'm feeling stronger now"; and "I have the mind-set of a champion."

Specific self-talk refers to those self-statements used to project and reaffirm particular skills, goals, and attributes. Examples are: "I enjoy the challenge of scuba diving, and the deeper the better"; "I'm giving law school my best effort and enjoying the process"; and "Public speaking comes naturally to me."

Process self-talk denotes one- or two-word self-statements that can be used as "trigger" ideas throughout the day or night, as well as during the actual performance of an activity. Some examples include: "Relax"; "Easy does it"; "Calm and confident"; and "Make it happen!"

For these three types of positive self-statements to be most effective, it is extremely important to construct and phrase them properly. Here are specific guidelines for you to use that will strengthen your ability to do this.

1. Make a conscious decision to turn negative self-talk into positive self-talk.

Listen to what you're saying and thinking in anticipation of and in response to your daily challenges. Become aware of your own negative self-talk and stop it in its tracks! I stop my own negative self-talk by saying to myself: "Bad seeds, Denis! Stop now!" Interestingly enough, when I *think* those words, my negative thoughts do stop. Then I construct affirmative self-talk statements in their place.

2. Don't allow others to contaminate your self-talk with their negativity.

Negative self-talk is often a habit of thinking that's been picked up from a family member, friend, or coworker. The next time someone offers you some of his or her negative statements, don't agree mentally. You can either ignore the comment and say nothing, or you can change the mood and try to help the speaker with your positive response to the comment.

For example, one day someone said to me, "Gee, Denis, 0you look tired and worn-out." And I responded, cheerfully, "Really? I'm surprised to hear that, because I'm feeling very relaxed and refreshed. I've been traveling a great deal and I'm in the renewal mode." Actually, I probably did look a little fatigued, but I felt better just answering that I was in the renewal mode.

3. Direct your self-talk toward what you want, instead of away from what you don't want.

For example, don't tell yourself, "I won't be late anymore." Say instead, "I always arrive early for appointments." Your mind can't concentrate on the reverse of an idea. If you state a proposition negatively, as in the example just given, your unconscious is merely going to receive words like *late* and *won't*. That's hardly what you intended. So promise yourself the condition you desire, without describing the condition you want to change. I like to write a self-statement for each of my major performance goals on a three-by-five-inch card. I always use the present tense, as if the objective had already been achieved. For example, "I am enjoying improving my fitness", or "I am attaining more knowledge of American history." I also use action modifiers such as "effortlessly," "calmly," "easily," and emotion words such as "enthusiastically," "happily," and "powerfully achieving my goal."

4. Keep your self-talk noncompetitive.

You can only control your own thoughts and your own actions. You can only do your best. You're not always going to emerge victorious over others. On some days, the competition will simply score more points. There's no reason to ever say to yourself something like, "If I don't get the promotion, I hope nobody does!" You're the one who will suffer the negative effects of that kind of thinking.

5. In constructing your self-statements, focus on incremental improvements.

Remember what we learned in Chapter One about breaking your goals down into bite-size pieces, and stair-stepping your way to the top. If you want to write a novel, don't think about trying to top *Moby Dick*. Focus on writing one or two pages a day.

* * *

Your self-suggestions can relate to any area of your life that you want to improve. Your brain is the computer, your body is the vehicle. Always remember that you have two people inside of you: the person you are now and the person you will surely become.

To sum up, here are the ground rules for making your self-statements highly effective:

- Your statements should always generate feelings of focus, confidence, strength, good health, and happiness.

- Write down your statements and read them twice a day. See yourself having already reached your goal. Allow yourself actually to feel the emotion. During the day visualize yourself going through the actual process of achieving your goal.

- Just before you perform, think about both your general and your specific positive self-statements. If you are about to play in a tennis match, you might be saying: "Today is my best day ever"; "I am calm, relaxed, and full of energy"; "I keep my eye on the ball at all times."

The Power of Self-transformation

Several years ago, *Life* magazine carried a story about the great actress Meryl Streep on the set of *Ironweed,* a bleak film in which she plays a ragged outcast during the Depression who dies in a cheap hotel room. For nearly an hour before the cameras rolled for the final scene, she hugged a giant bag of ice cubes to simulate the feeling of lifelessness. In the scene, her hobo lover, played by Jack Nicholson, cried and sobbed, shaking her body. During the filming and after the filming was completed, Meryl just lay there on the bed cold and still. The crew began to panic— she didn't appear to be breathing. After ten minutes, she began to emerge from a deep, trancelike state which she had deliberately entered.

"Now that," said the director, "is an actress."

According to Brad Darrach, author of the *Life* article, Streep looks, speaks, thinks, moves, and feels like the characters she plays. She is endowed with magnificent powers of self-transformation. Sydney Pollack, the Oscar-winning director, says that Meryl can actually vanish into another person. Director Mike Nichols agrees. "She changes who she is and casts a spell over other members of the cast. As she becomes the person she is portraying, the other actors begin to react to her as if she were that person. She changes the chemistry of all the relationships."

Like Meryl Streep, you—in real life—can look, think, move, feel, and *be* the roles you want to assume and the goals you want to achieve. You can literally become the person you're portraying.

The time to start is now.

CHAPTER SEVEN

Strength Through Mental Toughness

Out of the grandstand and into the winner's circle
Learn from the experts
Don't rush success
Listen to your body
No negative simulations
Focus on desired results
Expect the unexpected
The "Business Decathlon"
A mental-toughness checklist

Out of the Grandstand and into the Winner's Circle

A hush of anticipation settles over the Olympic stadium in Mexico City, where the attention of the huge crowd is firmly fixed on the high-jump bar. Bill Toomey, a former high school English teacher and the oldest athlete ever to compete in the decathlon, is preparing to make his jump as part of the ten-event, week-long competition that ends with the crowning of the greatest all-around athlete in the world. Four years ago he'd been among the spectators at the previous Olympiad. Now he's desperately trying to make it to the winner's circle.

The high jump is not Bill Toomey's best event. In the first event of the decathlon competition, Toomey had electrified the crowd by setting a record in the hundred-meter. But in so doing, he'd pulled a muscle. The injury handicaps him throughout the remainder of the competition.

Now, a German decathlon star has been steadily gaining points on Toomey and is expected to move ahead of him for good in the high jump. To make matters even worse for the injured American, rain begins to fall, soaking the tartan track, the grass infield, and the high-jump runway.

To succeed at such a moment, Bill Toomey needs something more than mere physical ability. He needs a kind of strength that few people understand. But he has that strength.

During the years of training leading up to this moment, he has forged it within himself.

As he stood there in the rain that afternoon in 1968, Bill Toomey thought back over the four years leading up to this one moment in Olympic history.

In 1964, in Tokyo, he had watched from the grandstand while German athletes finished first, third, and sixth in the decathlon. What did they know about preparation for this grueling series of events that the rest of the world didn't know?

Toomey headed for Germany to learn the answer to that question and to begin his long, uphill quest to become a champion. He was determined to become the first competitor in history to go from being a spectator in the stands to winning the decathlon gold medal in the following Olympiad.

In the course of achieving his goal, Toomey discovered that mental toughness is the ability to thrive on pain and adversity. In other words, ''When it starts to hurt, you start to win.'' This conversion of stumbling blocks into stepping stones is what truly sets the champion apart from the rest of society.

During the course of my many conversations with Bill Toomey, he and I have formulated some basic rules for developing the quality of mental toughness, as listed at the start of this chapter.

Let's take a closer look at each of these qualities that all winners share.

Learn from the Experts

This rule may seem obvious, but acting upon it may be deceptive.

In watching and training with the German athletes, Bill Toomey learned that he did not have good form in running the hurdles. The Germans suggested that by placing the hurdles eight yards apart, rather than the normal ten yards, he could improve on his form. That seemed unlikely to Toomey, who assumed the shorter distance would disrupt his timing. But he tried it anyway.

Why? Simply because his mentors had finished first, third, and sixth in the Olympics. He was the student, and they were the experts with indisputably proven records of success.

The result: Toomey discovered that, with the hurdles six feet closer together, he had no time to think and was forced to depend upon his reflexes. Sure enough, his form improved.

In addition to his German mentors, Bill Toomey also studied the techniques of a former world-record-holder in the high jump, Valery Brumel, a Russian. When Toomey learned refinements in technique that allowed him to increase his jumping height nearly four inches in two months, he observed, "I can't grow any taller, but I can always grow a lot smarter."

Bill Toomey made the transition from English teacher to Olympic aspirant to decathlon champion. You can improve the times in your own "decathlon" events, even if they're performed in a conference room instead of an Olympic stadium. Just as Bill

Toomey chose the German athletes as his mentors and role models, you can seek out successful individuals who can make you better at what you do.

Warren Bennis, professor at the University of Southern California Graduate School of Management, is one of the nation's leading experts on how to achieve managerial excellence and leadership. In his book *On Becoming a Leader,* Bennis describes how a successful executive in the film industry made the transition from a previous career doing government work in Washington.[1]

The aspiring moviemaker received permission from the head of a major studio simply to *watch* and *listen.* For months, the newcomer sat in the studio head's office, learning the Hollywood jargon, finding out how to agree and disagree, how to make suggestions, and how to give orders. Whenever he heard something he didn't understand, he wrote it down and asked someone about it later. While he was actually in the presence of the studio head, however, he simply became a "fly on the wall."

In this way, he transformed himself into a professional in just a few months. Simply being in the same room with a true insider brought the kind of practical knowledge he could never have obtained by academic study.

When you're in the presence of a genuine authority in your industry, think less about talking and more about listening. And when you hear something directed at you, take it seriously and act upon it. It will probably prove to be valuable advice, if it's spoken by someone whose credentials you know to be genuine.

The hurdles you're jumping over may not be the same kind Bill Toomey faced, but, like him, you need all the help you can get.

Don't Rush Success

Bill Toomey began his preparation for the 1968 Olympics four full years before the Games began.

"With four years to work with, you ought to be able to accomplish something, no matter what your goal," Toomey told me, with a laugh.

In 1964, Bill Toomey created a four-year plan for becoming a little better each day in all ten decathlon events. The goal was to reach peak performance just in time for the Mexico City competition.

As it turned out, however, during 1965 and 1966 he was forced to spend more than four months in the hospital with a serious case of mononucleosis and a liver infection, which nearly ended his athletic career. During his entire four-year training cycle, Toomey believes he only was actively training 50 percent of the time, due to his illnesses, two knee surgeries, several other operations, and radiation treatment for his liver problem.

In spite of all his setbacks and injuries, Toomey took the approach that a ten-sport Olympian has to conserve energy and go with the flow. He believed that impatience, frustration, and struggling before the 1968 Games would just create more injuries, more muscle pulls, and a martyr complex based on the feeling that he was up against overwhelming odds. So he stopped pushing so hard and played the cards he was dealt.

As I listened to Bill Toomey describe the importance of developing patience and acceptance of the problems that were beyond his control, I thought of some of my most treasured moments spent with one of my greatest mentors, the late author and social commentator Earl Nightingale.

Earl had invited me to join him for a day of fishing in his skiff near his home in Punta Gorda, Florida. The fish weren't biting, so we were philosophizing. Or, rather, Earl was philosophizing and I was listening.

Earl Nightingale was the most widely read person I had ever met. As we drifted there in the Gulf, he talked about the ancient Chinese wisdom of "going with the flow" or, in our situation, of not trying to row our boat against the tide.

From memory, Earl quoted Lao-tzu's classic book, the *Tao-te Ching*. He said that trying to force our way against the current was a sign of emotional and intellectual weakness.

"Bend with the wind," he said, "and you'll still be around when the hurricane passes and the good weather returns."

Earl Nightingale likened genuine mental toughness to the principles of the martial arts, where the aggressor's own power and force are used to defeat him. When an attacker makes a move, you simply channel him, using his force to cause him to lose balance and fall.

As only he could, Earl painted a verbal picture of the kind of person who smiles at adversity; a person who understands that goals are best achieved by going with the tide and with the wind, without force, anger, or impatience.

As we reeled in our lines and headed back to the private dock behind Earl's house, he looked at the water and remarked that, although it appears to be fluid and soft, in time it will wear away the largest, hardest rock. He said the paradox of toughness is that what appears aggressive and hard is in fact easily broken. What appears soft and patient is really strong.

Earl Nightingale and I didn't catch any fish that day, but I gained a boatful of memories, and truths to last a lifetime.

Listen to Your Body

As we continued our discussions of his preparation for the decathlon, Bill Toomey told me that his most accurate progress reports literally came from inside himself.

Again and again he would ask himself the questions: How do I feel about my progress today? Is my body signaling distress? Am I motivated toward my goals? Am I focused, or too easily distracted?

And finally, the most important questions of all: *Are my goals really my own? Are they realistic in terms of what I've done in the past and what I can do in the future?*

Only you can ask those questions in a genuinely meaningful way—and, what's more, only you can answer them.

No Negative Simulations

Why trust your own internal feedback more than that from coworkers, friends, or even family members? Because of Mental Toughness Rule Number 4: *No Negative Simulations.*

By negative simulations, I mean mentally rehearsing problems, exaggerating them or, worst of all, creating them out of thin air. When you indulge in negative simulation, you're joining what Bill Toomey calls the Bathtub Club.

During his competitive career, Toomey observed that when certain athletes noticed a minor injury, they proceeded to spend a great deal of time in the whirlpool bath. In Toomey's opinion, some people thrive on talking about their minor ailments and enjoy the attention they receive in therapy sessions. This is one reason why people with broken legs always love to have their friends come by and sign their plaster casts. Unfortunately, the pleasure derived from that kind of sympathy can lead to seeking attention for negative reasons.

Although he always listened carefully to his body's responses, Bill Toomey had a cardinal rule of never talking about a problem or injury. If he had to put ice on a muscle pull, or consult with a doctor, he did so in private, kept it to himself, and tried not to focus on daily ups and downs.

During his final preparations for the Olympics, he even stopped checking his times, heights, and distances. Toomey didn't want to evaluate each and every performance. That, he said, would be like a farmer who digs up his seeds every day to see how they're doing.

Like it or not, you are going to have some good days and some bad days. The ability to make the most of the good days is a fundamental quality of mental toughness. Conversely, a tendency toward negative simulations is much more likely to keep you in the "Bathtub Club" than in the winner's circle.

Focus on Desired Results

Winners dwell on the rewards of success. Losers focus on the penalties of failure. Winners imagine the solid weight of the gold medal around their necks. They imagine the roar of the crowd in the stadium.

But there's much more to focusing than visualizing the future award ceremony.

Most of Bill Toomey's focus was on the present. He knew that if you concentrate on the present, you eliminate what happened yesterday and any apprehension over what may happen tomorrow. In other words, two thirds of your worries automatically disappear!

One of the ways champions get into the peak performance

zone is by approaching each day as a whole new event, with the past forgotten. But if you're going to compete in the week-long, ten-event Olympic decathlon, you had better focus also on the event in the future.

Toomey had a very creative method of positive psychological programming to help him peak at the ideal moment. He hung a large calendar on the wall, and put big circles around each of the major national championships leading to the Olympic Games in Mexico City.

As it happened, there were five crucial events, including the Olympic qualifying meet. As he circled the five dates, he also silently told his mind and body to be ready for victory at that moment.

Soon, all by themselves, the circled dates became his vision of the five rings that comprise the Olympic logo.

Expect the Unexpected

Bill Toomey called this Contingency Planning. I call it: Expect the Best, Plan for the Worst, and Be Prepared For a Surprise. It was this final rule of mental toughness that won Toomey the decathlon gold medal and a place in Olympic history.

During his four years of preparation, Toomey had always planned for the unexpected. At his workouts at the University of California at Santa Barbara, when the temperature was eighty degrees, he always brought his special track shoes for rainy weather. Of course, rainy days are rare in Santa Barbara, but Toomey was planning for every contingency. He always prepared for every conceivable physical, mental, and meteorological possibility.

He was one of the few who did. On the rare occasions when it did rain during practice, he noticed that all the other athletes would seek shelter under an awning or move inside the gym. But Bill Toomey would practice in the rain, just in case it rained in Mexico City.

And on that late, rainy October afternoon at seventy-three hundred feet in the Mexico City stadium, I sat there, holding my breath, watching Bill Toomey duel with the German champion for the gold medal. The German appeared anxious and a little annoyed with the condition of the runway. He missed at a height much lower than his best.

Bill Toomey was relaxed, calm, and looked like he was playing outside in the rain. The oldest man ever to compete in the Olympic decathlon soared six feet, six inches in the rain. He walked away with the gold medal.

Today he says, "I'm still totally amazed by the whole experience. There are people who warn about not having false hope, but I believe false hope is far less dangerous than having low expectations. I came out of the grandstand in 1964 at the Tokyo Olympics, and went after my fantasy of competing in Mexico four years later. Yet I'm a guy who looks more like a piano tuner or an Arthur Murray dance instructor than a decathlon winner."

In 1990, before the Goodwill Games in the Pacific Northwest, Bill Toomey and other former champions spoke to the new U.S. decathlon hopefuls. Did their stories of mental toughness make an impression? Apparently they did. A short time later, at the nationals, the new decathletes had the highest point totals scored by any Americans during the past fifteen years.

The "Business Decathlon"

Physically, the Malcolm Baldridge National Quality Award is a not-very-large glass statuette. Symbolically, it is the highest honor attainable by an American company. To win, a company must convince a blue-ribbon panel that it produces the highest quality products in the nation.

As John Hillkirk and Gary Jacobson recount in their book *Grit, Guts, and Genius: True Tales of Mega-Success*, sixty-six companies competed for the Baldridge Award in 1988. Most of the entries were actually divisions of large corporations such as IBM, Kodak, and Hewlett-Packard. But the winner was Motorola—the whole company, not just a division.[2]

Motorola's quest for the award began in 1981, with scout teams being dispatched to outstanding manufacturing organizations around the world. The goal was not only to see how they did it, but to see how it could be done *better*.

As part of this effort, all Motorola employees were challenged to reduce drastically the number of defects in their work. Hourly workers were made responsible for identifying mistakes, and were rewarded for doing so. Engineers designing cellular phones reduced the number of parts per phone from 1,378 to 523. The result: Defects were reduced by no less than 90 percent. But Motorola still wasn't satisfied.

New goals were set. For cellular phones, it was 3.4 defects per one million parts produced. That would translate to 99.9997 percent of all phones produced being defect-free.

All Motorola employees received wallet-size cards stating the company's goals. A videotape was produced to explain why error-free quality of 99 percent wasn't good enough. The video pointed out that, if everyone in the country operated at 99 percent quality, there would be two hundred thousand wrong drug prescriptions each year, to say nothing of thirty thousand newborn babies accidentally dropped by doctors or nurses. Would 99 percent quality be good enough for the police officers who entrusted their lives to Motorola radios?

By the time the actual judging for the Baldridge Award took place, Motorola products had achieved a level of quality that made the competition a walkover.

But was it worth it?

For winning a gold medal, an Olympic athlete gets an unforgettable moment of glory. Whether or not he reaps millions in product endorsements, that moment is something he can take pride in for the rest of his life. A company, however, can't sustain a supreme level of commitment based on a foot-high statue in a top executive's office.

Fortunately, there were plenty of rewards where it counted: on the bottom line. In 1988, Motorola was able to save two hundred fifty million dollars by eliminating costly repairs and replacements. Revenues increased 23 percent, and profits rose 44 percent to an all-time record high.

Moreover, morale soared throughout the company. A Motorola executive declared, "Winning the Baldridge Award had an effect that money just can't buy."

The lesson here is that you don't have to be able to jump high or run fast to experience the exhilaration of being the best at what you do. You just have to want to work hard and work well.

Following are some action reminders to help you develop mental toughness in everything you do.

A Mental-Toughness Checklist

1. Learn everything you can about winners who have overcome setbacks and handicaps in order to become successful.

By realizing that failure and disappointment have not deterred the great champions in every field throughout history, you'll gain the courage and motivation to pursue your own dreams. Think also about the millions of winners you may never have heard or read about—winners like my friend Carol Marshall. In a letter to me she said that, long ago and far away, as a high school senior, she wanted to be a golf professional, but her career took a different path. She played lots of local tournament golf, got married, had four children, became a single parent, worked as a school counselor for twenty-something years, taught seminars at the University of Wisconsin in Superior—and, not too long ago, began teaching golf. Much to her surprise and delight, she learned that there is a teaching division of the Ladies Professional Golf Association; today she is a card-carrying professional golfer, just like she dreamed about in high school more than forty years ago.

2. Don't embrace the idea that you need to "come from behind" in order to get ahead.

Learn from the trials and tribulations of others, but do not force yourself into unrealistically high expectations. Be sure that you understand the difference between "No pain, no gain" and "Patience, Pacing, and Persistence." You don't need to experience physical or emotional pain in order to succeed. That's a dangerous myth that can lead to emotional burnout and physical exhaustion.

3. Give solution-oriented feedback when problem-solving.

Don't dwell on what went wrong. Instead, focus on what to do next. Winners believe that they have the inner resources to survive any number of setbacks on the way to achieving their goals. They don't waste time studying the damage they may have sustained after encountering a disappointment. It may sound corny, but it's really true that "you aren't beat until the moment you stop trying." Only you can determine when that moment has arrived.

4. Get comfortable with the unfamiliar.

Break your daily routines. Put your TV set in a closet for a month. Try a new restaurant. Drive to work using a different highway or street. Make at least one new friend each month, even though not every one of them is likely to become a lifelong buddy. Remember, too, that you can explore new territory emotionally as well as physically. Try to become aware of your ups and downs, of what makes you happy and what makes you sad, and make an effort to be less of a victim of your moods.

5. Think and speak well of your health.

Teach yourself and your children to use positive self-talk about fitness. Too much attention paid to minor health irritations may unconsciously suggest that there's some value in being ill. Also, we've come to believe that we're surrounded by chemicals, electrical currents, and mysterious rays that make going out the door a life-threatening experience. Certainly there is much to be concerned about, but it's just as certain that the world is now much safer to your health than ever before. In 1918, the influenza epidemic killed more Americans than died in World War I. In the 1950s, polio was a real threat to every child in the country. I'm not suggesting that you shouldn't take care of your health. I'm just pointing out the benefits of seeing things in a positive perspective.

6. Verify before you glorify.

Don't be a victim of the ads and the fads. The world is full of greedy people trying to put you (or your money) in their pockets. When you encounter something in the media that seems to impress you, check the source. Call the research department of a national publication you trust or a major university you respect.

7. Join with individuals who have already achieved their goals or who are dedicated to goals similar to yours.

Avoid associating with people who have the same unresolved problems or who are frustrated by their lack of achievements. Mental toughness means neither going it alone nor trusting in erroneous "quick-fix" formulas. Mental toughness *does* mean learning from the "pros" who have been there many times before.

8. Above all, never forget that the real secret of mental toughness is contingency planning.

Expect the best, plan for the worst, and prepare to be surprised. You can't control what others do. But you can anticipate the various alternatives and prepare for them as best you can. You can also control your responses to what happens. Like Bill Toomey, practice in the rain—and bring along your rainy-day running shoes even when the sun is shining. *Especially* when the sun is shining!

CHAPTER EIGHT

The "Coachability" Factor

Dear Mr. Waitley . . .
The three components of leadership
The other qualities of a winning coach
The most coachable person I've ever met
A puppy becomes a bulldog

Dear Mr. Waitley . . .

Thank you for everything you have taught me about success in your tapes and books. Before I began to read and to listen to them, I was worried about my dreams and goals and thought they were useless. For the past year and seven months I was seriously ill with a condition I thought I'd be stuck with for the rest of my life. I've learned to change my thoughts and set goals and today I'm almost completely recovered.

Sir, I'm only sixteen, but I want to become the world's youngest and most successful entrepreneur. To make this goal a reality, I carry around 3-by-5 index cards with me, watch new and innovative TV programs, and read new magazines to become a trend spotter, just as you advised. I also remembered what you said about not giving up after failure, how to build a team of supporters and not to rest on my laurels.

Mr. Waitley, I realize you're a very busy man, but I've

enclosed a list of questions for you, with spaces for your answers, and a postage-paid self-addressed envelope for your convenience. I hope one day to meet you and shake your hand. Thank you for reading my letter and answering my questions.

Recently, I received the above personal letter from a teenager in New England.

I was happy to get it, because one of the greatest mistakes young people or beginners in any field can make is to be afraid of asking for help. They don't realize that even the so-called experts are pleased when someone genuinely wants to know their opinion.

At first glance, this letter might not seem directly related to our study of the new dynamics of winning. But certainly *coaching* can be an important component of success, in athletics and everywhere else. As I read the questions that formed the remainder of the letter, I recognized an opportunity to engage in some long-distance coaching in the always challenging game of life.

Here are a few of the questions.

Do you have a favorite success quote?

Actually, I have many, but I gave her two: "Losers let it happen, winners make it happen," and, "It's not who you are that holds you back, it's what you think you're not."

The first quote emphasizes the fact that winners are naturally action-oriented people. They see themselves as *actors* in the world's arena, not as passive objects or victims being *acted upon*.

Even when they fail, winners fail in an active way. If you have to fail, fail big. That's the way successful people approach everything they do.

I think one of the most important events in modern sports history occurred in 1964, when Joe Namath predicted that his team, the New York Jets of the American Football League, would defeat the National Football League's Baltimore Colts in Super Bowl III.

At the time, this prediction seemed totally outrageous for several reasons.

First, the Colts were favored by nineteen points. Second, in the first two Super Bowls, the AFL's team had been easily defeated by the NFL representative.

But the most striking thing about Namath's prediction was that things like that simply weren't being done at that time. Athletes just weren't talking that way. In addition to feeling surprised when the Jets won, I personally felt a sense of relief—because the whole country was ready to crush Namath for his audacity in shooting his mouth off like that. It seemed like he would have had to move to South America, if not Siberia, if the Jets lost.

As it turned out, Namath had started a trend.

Several years later, before his fight with Joe Frazier, Muhammad Ali made a Namath-like prediction of victory. Once again, this sort of bravado seemed outrageous. Early in his career, Ali used to make predictions about his matches, but at that point he was competing against fighters who were clearly less talented than himself. Now Ali hadn't even been in the ring for several years, and Frazier was the undefeated champion. But Ali continued to guarantee his victory. He didn't just say it once, either. He must have said it dozens of times, and at least half the time he said it in verse.

This time the prediction was wrong. Ali lost. It was a close fight, he fought hard, but he lost.

Shortly thereafter Ali was scheduled to be a guest on Johnny Carson's television talk show. Just before he was introduced, I wondered how the audience would react when he came onstage. After all, here was a man who had really shot his mouth off. He had *absolutely guaranteed* that he was going to win, and then he lost. It was embarrassing.

When Ali came out, however, he literally received a standing ovation.

Instead of being viewed as a man who'd made a fool out of

himself, he was treated like someone who had courageously put his reputation on the line. The fact that it didn't turn out the way he'd said was much less important than his willingness to risk *big*.

Since the days of Namath and Ali, of course, that kind of athlete's bragging ritual has been totally devalued, to the point where it means nothing whatsoever. But, for me at least, it provided an opportunity to learn that if you've got the guts to *say* you're in control of your own destiny, the world will respect you for it, even if events prove you were wrong.

The second quote—"It's not who you are that holds you back, it's what you think you're not"—reminds me of a very important concept I came across while doing some of my research on behavioral psychology. It's a concept known as *learned helplessness*.

Here's how learned helplessness operates.

Suppose you started working for a company that had weekly staff meetings every Monday morning. One of the purposes of the meetings was for people to make suggestions about how things could be done more efficiently. But suppose that whenever you made a suggestion you got shouted down by everybody around the table. After a while you would probably feel a little less eager to present your ideas, wouldn't you? In fact, there's an excellent chance that before very long you would simply stop saying anything at all.

Worst of all, even if you went to work for an entirely different organization, the chances are you would *still* be reluctant to assert yourself because of what happened in those other staff meetings. You'd have internalized those negative experiences and turned them into negative ideas about yourself. You'd think, *I'm not somebody who people want to listen to.*

You'd have "learned" to feel helpless, even in situations where there's no evidence to justify that feeling.

Instead of focusing on what they're not, winners look at

what they *are* and at the positive contributions that they're determined to make. What happened yesterday was a function of the conditions that were in effect yesterday. As the saying goes: "That was then, this is now."

Who are the people—past or present—whom you most admire?

I was able to provide quite a long list, beginning with Jesus Christ, my wife Susan, my grandmother, Benjamin Franklin, Mother Teresa, Thomas Edison, Abraham Lincoln, Jonas Salk, and many others. It was almost impossible to rank them, because I've been fortunate to have so many mentors.

Edison, of course, made many valuable discoveries, but to me none is more important than his definition of genius as "two percent inspiration and ninety-eight percent perspiration." Edison also had some great insights into the reasons why people fail to achieve their goals. He said, "Failure is really a matter of conceit. People don't work hard because, in their conceit, they imagine they'll succeed without ever making an effort. Most people believe that they'll wake up some day and find themselves rich. Actually, they've got it half right, because eventually they do 'wake up.' "[1]

As long as there are inquisitive, eager-to-learn, coachable young people out there, I'll be available to try to be a good coach.

The Three Components of Leadership

Understanding the qualities of a good coach will help you motivate your employees, support your friends, and brighten your family relationships. It will also help you become more "coachable."

Two of the nation's top sports psychologists, Dr. Bruce Ogilvie and Dr. Thomas Tutko, whom I referred to earlier, have studied the characteristics of sixty-four outstanding athletic coaches. Their discoveries are well worth reviewing because the subjects were individuals who have gained considerable prominence in either professional or amateur competition.

The first characteristic of winning coaches was that, as athletes, most of them were exceptionally *coachable* themselves.

This quality of "being coachable" has three important aspects:

First, the coachable performer respects the role of authority figures. This is usually the result of previous positive experiences with parents and teachers. Respect and trust for authority, however, does not mean "blind submission" and robotlike conformity. The coachable champion trusts his or her own judgment as well as the decisions of designated leaders.

Second, in addition to the ability to accept guidance from others, coachable performers have a healthy personal impulse toward self-direction and freedom of interpretation. This means he or she enjoys innovation, and has the capacity to form new or different opinions from those held by other people.

This positive-quality self-direction shouldn't be confused with its destructive look-alike, which is the need to protest or rebel against authority. Many high-performance athletes and performers who showboat, display bizarre or immature behavior, and generally act up are really deceiving themselves, the media, and the public into believing they are merely seeking self-expression. Unfortunately, these individuals have a subconscious feeling that all authority figures will ultimately rob them of their freedom of action and choice. Most likely, they've grown up in the kind of environment that engenders an automatic defensive reaction against any form of structured atmosphere.

The third quality of a coachable person is a high tolerance for order and organization. Training schedules, practice routines, and other sometimes bothersome daily requirements are taken in stride, if not actually welcomed. This is in contrast to the disorganized competitor, who finds life overwhelming, and to the overly compulsive performer who is unable to adapt to any change in routine.

In summary, individuals who have a pattern of low respect for authority, low capacity for organization, and an exaggerated need for freedom and self-direction, present the greatest coaching challenge. They're also extremely unlikely to become effective leaders themselves, as the study by Dr. Ogilvie and Dr. Tutko demonstrated.

I have to admit, however, that there are exceptions to the rule that outstanding coaches were very coachable. One of the most striking exceptions is Mike Ditka, who has compiled a great record as coach of the Chicago Bears.

When Ditka was a player for the Bears in the early 1960s, he was absolutely fearless about standing up to George Halas, the owner-coach of the team and one of the founding fathers of the National Football League.

While negotiating a new contract with Halas, Ditka told reporters that Halas was so cheap, he tossed around nickels as if they were manhole covers. While other players accepted Halas's tongue-lashings in stoic silence, Ditka insisted on saying exactly what was on his mind. Despite Ditka's obvious greatness as a player, Halas eventually got fed up and traded him.

Yet in 1982, when the Bears' head coaching job opened up, George Halas insisted on hiring Mike Ditka. What's more, as Halas lay on his deathbed, Ditka was one of the few people he agreed to see. He declared that Ditka would take the Bears to the Super Bowl within three years, and that is exactly what happened.

Yes, all great coaches were themselves very coachable. Except the ones who weren't.

The Other Qualities of a Winning Coach

The study revealed these other qualities of successful coaches, in addition to their ability to accept direction and authority:

- Without exception, winning coaches are *success-driven,* with an intense need to come out on top. Moreover, they believe they *will* come out on top in the end, regardless of any setbacks encountered along the way.

- Winning coaches are orderly and organized individuals, who habitually plan ahead and who are naturally oriented toward the future. They don't "replay yesterday's game" in their heads; they prefer to focus on the games yet to be played.

- They are outgoing and warm, enjoying the company of others. In temperament, they seem unusually well equipped for managing their emotions under stress.

- Perhaps most important of all, winning coaches exhibit the highest level of emotional and intellectual *endurance* of any group of individuals that has been similarly studied. It appears that "stick-to-it-iveness" is the most prominent feature of the personality of successful coaches.

The Most Coachable Person I've Ever Met

The most coachable person I've ever met is my friend Harvey Mackay, whom I mentioned in an earlier chapter. His hugely successful books, *Swim with the Sharks* and *Beware the Naked Man,* have set sales records that may stand for years to come.

But Harvey is much more than simply a best-selling writer.

He's also CEO of a major corporation, an internationally renowned speaker, a prominent civic leader, a marathoner, and one of the top amateur tennis players in his home state of Minnesota. With good reason, *Fortune* magazine called Harvey ''Mr. Make-Things-Happen.''

One of Harvey's secrets is that he actively seeks out and allows himself to be coached by champions. He explains, ''You don't have to know everything, as long as you know people who know the things you don't. There's a lot that I don't know, so I shamelessly ask for advice.'' Harvey Mackay may well be the premier advice-seeker, advice-implementer, and, more recently, the best *advice-giver* in the country.

Beginning with Ping-Pong lessons at age 7, Harvey Mackay has developed an insatiable appetite to master everything he tackles. He took boxing lessons, dancing lessons, tennis lessons, and public-speaking lessons. Even today, receiving a minimum honorarium of twenty thousand dollars per keynote address, he still retains a speech coach, because Harvey understands there's always room for improvement in everything you do.

He is one of the few business writers and speakers to have toured the Soviet Union by invitation of Soviet business and government leaders. While several other of our colleagues have made the same trip, including Tom Peters and Mark McCormack, author of *What They Don't Teach You at Harvard Business School,* there was definitely a unique feature to Harvey Mackay's lecture: The first seven minutes of his talk were delivered by Harvey in Russian! And, knowing him as I do, I'm sure his Russian was near-perfect.

In addition to his Russian-language lessons, Harvey has also studied Chinese, Japanese, and Arabic.

Why does he do it? First, no one ever told him he couldn't or shouldn't. Second, his dad taught him to learn as much as he can and then find others who know even more. And, third, Harvey believes you should learn as much as humanly possible about your customer, your industry, and your profession.

What is the Harvey Mackay "coachability" program? Let's take a case in point. Suppose you want to run a marathon, but you're well into middle age and tennis is more your game than distance running. No problem. In the sections that follow, we'll take a look at how Harvey Mackay proceeds. By following his methodical approach, you can achieve greater success not just in running, but in everything you do.

1. Check your limits (if any).

Before you begin running marathons, get a complete medical workup from your physician. This should include a stress test and an evaluation of all factors relevant to your cardiovascular condition.

Then, get an expert assessment of your potential.

If the planned activity is a physical one, like running, there are sports medicine facilities throughout the country that can evaluate your aptitude for any sport, using tests similar to the ones performed by computer on your automobile. Using high-speed cinematography and computer simulation, it can be determined in advance whether you will be able to meet the demands of a given physical activity. This type of biomechanical profiling is standard throughout our entire Olympic movement. You can use it, at any age, to determine your strengths and weaknesses before attempting a new sport.

2. Get a personal coach.

When Harvey Mackay decided to begin training to run a marathon, he found out who the great local marathoners were. Then he found out who was considered to be the best coach. Then he hired him, and set up a three-month program to work personally with the coach.

This procedure works for virtually any activity, hobby, or profession. If you want to learn it, there's someone available for one-on-one or group sessions to train you.

3. Enroll in a class.

Both Harvey Mackay and I have enrolled in more classes than we can remember.

For his distance-running needs, Harvey enrolled in a class for marathoners. Recently, I enrolled in a class to learn how to play the piano by computer simulation.

My daughter Lisa went to Taiwan to study Mandarin Chinese. My daughter Deborah teaches communication skills to executives. Another daughter, Kim, enrolled in a class on how to export fashion merchandise. One of my sons, Darren, enrolled in a class on how to make video family documentaries and video portraits. When do you graduate from college? I hope never! School is never out for the winner. Education is a life-long process.

When you enroll in a class, get your money's worth. Never take a seat in the back of the room. Winners sit up front. From the first row, you can interact with the instructor, see and hear from the best vantage point, be noticed when you raise your hand, and be in a position to ask more personal questions immediately following the session.

If tape recorders are allowed, always tape the classes or meetings you attend. If not, find out if there is an audio- or videotape available of the class. Replay the tapes several times to internalize the material.

Take plenty of notes. Many of the most coachable people I know carry a journal with them at all times. They put a date at the top of each daily page in a book of lined paper and fill it in day by day. In this way, they have a running account of important notes and thoughts before, during, and after meetings, and throughout the day.

As a manager, you should encourage your employees to attend work-related conferences and seminars. And when I say *encourage*, that should include willingness to help defray the costs. Then, when the employee returns, you should ask him or her to submit a brief report on what was learned. You might even ask the attendee to give a miniseminar within your own company.[2]

4. The reader's edge.

Quite simply, the people who read the most are the most successful, regardless of occupation.

I've said this again and again throughout the years. I know Harvey Mackay agrees, because in learning to run a marathon he bought several books covering both the mental and physical aspects of the race.

I make it a point to read one nonfiction book each week and one fiction book each month. My weekly nonfiction reading increases my knowledge, my general awareness of changes and trends in the world, and strengthens my vocabulary. My monthly fiction reading sharpens my creative skills, enhances my vocabulary, and opens up my mind to new points of view. If your time is scarce, subscribe to *Executive Book Summaries,* in Bristol, Vermont. You'll get the key points from the national best-sellers at a glance. Also, listen to books on tape during commute time.

5. Network with winners in the field you are pursuing.

When I say *network,* I mean socially and informally. Harvey Mackay believes you can learn as much about marathoning or any other subject by socializing with the experts in a given field.

Why? It's simple. You pick up pointers on new eating and exercise habits. You learn about different training techniques. You hear about pitfalls and mistakes that can be avoided by preplanning. You hear positive stories of people like yourself who have transformed their dreams into reality. You learn about new equipment, new recreation ideas, and how to combine travel, friendship, and fitness.

6. Use television as a learning experience.

Harvey Mackay began exploring television and cable listings for marathons on television. He also rented videos on different aspects of running. He watched for newscasts that covered local and national road races to learn who, what, where, when, and how.

In my own profession and hobbies, I use cable channels, NOVA, PBS, satellite channels, and educational videocassettes to supplement my reading, audio listening, social networking, personal instruction, and class attendance. The public library is also one of my favorite spots to hang out.

7. Learn how to cross-train.

Harvey Mackay said cross-training helped him put the finishing touches on becoming a good marathoner. He utilized both an indoor and outdoor bicycle. Cycling is easier on the joints, muscles, and bones than running. It also provides variety to the training routine, and allows you the flexibility of all types of weather conditions.

You can cross-train for any sport, any hobby, or any career. Step back and think about the process, then find a second or third activity that requires the same type of training in a different environmental setting.

Harvey told me that by following these seven steps, running a respectable marathon was a piece of cake. He makes writing a national best-seller look like writing a letter to a friend. That's because he uses the same thorough approach to everything he does. The only thing that really bothers me about most-coachable Harvey is that he usually ends up doing much better than his coaches!

A Puppy Becomes a Bulldog

Before he had his dream season in 1988—twenty-three wins, sixty consecutive scoreless innings pitched, the Cy Young Award, and World Series' Most Valuable Player—Orel Hershiser had struggled as a rookie pitcher with the Los Angeles Dodgers. No one consulted him about strategy or what pitch to throw in a certain situation. In fact, he was getting the reputation of not being able to come through with the good pitch, even when he knew which one he was supposed to throw.

Because of his thin build, glasses, and boyish looks, people just assumed he had no fire in his belly. Yes, he had lots of potential. Everyone said that. But then they'd add, "He's just too nice."

Making things even more difficult for Hershiser was his defensiveness toward loud, brash Dodger manager Tommy Lasorda. Orel was sure he was on very thin ice and that any day Lasorda would send him back to the minor leagues. Little wonder then that Orel's heart hit his shoes when Tommy called him in for a personal chat.

Hershiser felt like he was headed for the principal's office. When an unsmiling Lasorda waved him to a chair, he knew he wasn't there to be congratulated on his pitcher's report card. Lasorda sat on the edge of his desk, looking down on his rookie pitcher, who stared back, unblinking, determined to agree with whatever his manager said.

"I want to talk to you about your mental approach to pitching," Lasorda began.

He seemed calm enough. Orel nodded as Lasorda recalled a game he had pitched a day or two before against Houston. Jose Cruz, a dangerous hitter with men on base, had come up with two outs and two men on base. His voice rising slightly, Lasorda moved closer and continued. "Cruz knows you can't afford to walk him, so he's sittin' on your three and one pitch. And what do you do?"

Lasorda is nose to nose now, and answers his own question: "You laid the ball in for him. Boom! He hits a double and two runs come in!"

"He thinks I'm hopeless," thought Hershiser. "I'm headed for the minors."

But what Lasorda said next didn't send Orel Hershiser to the minors. Instead, he sent him a message that changed him into a winning pitcher:

"You don't believe in yourself. You're scared to pitch to big-league hitters. But you've got the talent. If you didn't, I wouldn't have brought you up. Quit being so careful! Go after the hitter! Get ahead in that count!"

As Orel sat through his manager's stern lecture, one thing registered: Lasorda believed he had "good stuff." Maybe there was hope after all! Then Tommy Lasorda put in the clincher. Later, Lasorda would call this his Sermon on the Mound.

He told his promising, but ineffective, rookie: "If I could get a heart surgeon in here, I'd have him open my chest, take out my heart, and put it in your chest. You'd be in the Hall of Fame! If I had your stuff, I would have been in the Hall of Fame! I want you, starting today, to believe you're the best pitcher in baseball. I want you to look at that hitter and say, *There's no way you can ever hit me!* You've gotta believe that you can get anybody out who walks up there. Take charge! Be a bulldog out there. That's gonna be your new name: *Bulldog!*"[3]

Orel Hershiser left Tommy Lasorda's office both humbled and glowing inside. His manager knew he had big-league stuff. He belonged on the mound every bit as much as those hitters belonged in the batter's box. He didn't exactly like the idea of being called "Bulldog" Hershiser, but he'd have to live with it.

If he had been uncoachable, Hershiser would probably have faded back into oblivion, sulking because nobody understood him. The uncoachable player doesn't sit unflinching when his manager tells it like it is. Instead, he lashes out, refusing to listen to or respect authority.

But Orel Hershiser was coachable. He took his manager's advice and the rest is recorded in some of the most exciting pages in Dodger history. Just two days later, he came out of the bullpen with a sore arm and pitched three strong innings. Soon he was in the starting rotation, pitching complete games, and chalking up shutouts. He started winning because he became a believer.

He became a believer not just because Tommy Lasorda had given him the "Sermon on the Mound." He became a believer because he was adaptable, because he was willing to listen openly to criticism, no matter how uncomfortable it felt. And his ego was strong enough to sit quietly and not strike back in protest.

And as the consummate *coachable* champion, Orel Hershiser made the transition from gentle puppy into big league "Bulldog."

The Quality of Leadership

What Is a Leader?

Real leaders come in all shapes and sizes and from all walks of life. But they all have a few things in common:

They are never so big that they can't bend down to help someone else.

They are never so wise that they don't remember who taught them.

They are never so gifted that they won't share their skills with others.

They are never so fearless that they don't play by the rules and live by the law.

And they are never such big winners that they forget what it feels like to lose.

That description of a leader was inspired by a speech given by the venerable film actor James Stewart at a benefit dinner a few years ago.

I really like simple definitions like that. But today there are so many books, tapes, and seminars on leadership that it's difficult to sort out whether anything really new is being said. I suspect that authentic leadership has always been the same. But because it isn't practiced all that often either at work or at home, it can seem like the whole idea of leadership is new.

For twenty years, my friend and fellow author Chris Hegarty has said the goal of most so-called leaders has been to convince people to think more of them. On the other hand, the goal of the authentic leader is to cause people to think more of themselves. Authentic leadership is a very simple principle that most people try to make complicated.

One Moment That Saved a Career

Nearly a half-century ago, Jackie Robinson made history when he became the first black baseball player to break into the major leagues by joining the Brooklyn Dodgers. The owner of the Dodgers at the time was Branch Rickey. He told Robinson, "It'll be tough. You're going to take abuse you never dreamed of. But if you're willing to try it, I'll back you all the way."

And Rickey was right. Jackie Robinson was abused verbally and physically, especially by opposing runners sliding into his position at second base. He was subjected to a steady barrage of racial slurs from the crowd, from the players on the other teams in the league, and even from members of his own team.

One day, Robinson was having it particularly tough out on the field. He had bobbled two ground balls. A roar of boos cascaded from the crowd. Then, in full view of thousands of spectators, Pee Wee Reese, the Dodger shortstop and team captain, called a time-out.

He looked at the crowd, then walked over to Robinson and said, "Don't worry, partner, you're a real pro. Everything's going to be just fine real soon. Take my word for it."

Robinson, of course, became one of the most outstanding players ever to wear a major-league uniform. Years later he reflected on that brief conversation at second base: "Pee Wee Reese made me feel like I belonged. That one moment may have saved my career."

It seems so simple, doesn't it? Executives and managers want the respect of their employees—but what they should want is for their employees to respect themselves. Parents want the love and admiration of their children. What they should want is for their children to feel good about who they are and confident about what they can do.

It's never easy to be one of the newest members of a team, a company, or even a family. Feeling like a fifth wheel is always uncomfortable. As a leader, be sensitive to opportunities for welcoming someone who feels estranged, to accept the differences in others who work and live nearby, and to see the other person's point of view before passing judgment. A real leader appreciates the differences among individuals, and finds value in those differences that enhance all our lives.

Opportunities, Not Obligations

Leadership isn't based on theory or technique. It depends on your ability to subordinate your own ego for the good of the team.

Authentic leaders listen and learn. They ask questions before they offer opinions.

The old-fashioned, control-oriented, authoritarian leaders are soon going to appear on the endangered species list. They try to get what they want with power and aggressiveness. They think fear-based motivation tactics succeed brilliantly. But while their subordinates hurry to do their bidding for the moment, deep resentments are being created. The short-term gains of the dictator-style leader actually represent disaster in the making.

The authentic leader may appear naïve in being uncritically open to whatever emerges in a group setting. This openness is much more powerful than any system of judgments ever devised. By being open and honest, the real leader attracts a like response from his or her associates.

In the previous chapter, I recalled how moved I was when Earl Nightingale spoke of an ancient book of Oriental philosophy during our afternoon of fishing in Florida. That same book, the *Tao-te Ching*, has some important insights into the nature of true leadership:

> The Master has no mind of her own.
> She works with the mind of the people.
> She is good to people who are good.
> She is also good to people who aren't good . . .
> She trusts people who are trustworthy.
> She also trusts people who aren't trustworthy . . .[1]

Good leadership motivates others to their highest levels by offering opportunities, not obligations. It's a paradox that the best leaders are really the best followers. The wise leader doesn't always grab the front-and-center spotlight or the gavel, but stays more in the background, or at the side of the conference table.

Many of the greatest accomplishments of a true leader go largely unrecognized. Because the true leader doesn't push, manipulate, or control, there's no resentment among team members and little resistance. Things just seem to get accomplished without all the rushing and crushing of emotions. When a leader gives up trying to impress the group, he or she becomes very impressive.

Please don't misinterpret: By being open, caring, and non-judgmental, leaders don't have to be too vulnerable, too sentimental, or too ambivalent to make decisions and take charge where necessary. A real leader leads by listening first and then sparks the internal values in others to gain decisive movement toward accomplishing the common goals. In many instances, this open, warm, and gentle style of leadership is ingrained in us from early childhood.

That's why it is so important for parents to be authentic leaders of their children, so that the children in turn can grow up to be real leaders in society.

A Lesson from Luciano Pavarotti

Many years ago, there was a young boy who wanted desperately to become an opera singer. His parents paid for his lessons, just as many parents today pay for music and dance lessons. But, through the early years, his teacher gave him no hope of ever becoming a professional. "Son," the teacher told him, "you sound like the wind in the shutters!"

Still, the boy's mother believed in her son. She had been to his recitals and had listened as he practiced in his room day after day. So she sent him to another, more experienced, teacher. To pay for the cost of her son's lessons, she often went without shoes—sometimes even without food. The boy was Enrico Caruso, and he became the greatest tenor of his time—because his mother listened to him and helped lead him to develop his talent.[2]

Many years after Enrico Caruso, there was another boy who could sing. His father wanted him to be a professional singer and his mother thought he should pursue the more secure profession of teaching. Wanting to please both his parents, he devoted himself to both fields. He took singing lessons while growing up in Modena, Italy, and enrolled in teachers' college at the same time.

Upon graduation, he approached his father for career counseling: "Father, shall I be a teacher or a singer?" "Luciano," his father said, "if you try to sit in two chairs, you will fall between them. In life, *you* must choose one chair."[3]

We all know which choice Luciano Pavarotti made. After seven more years of study, practice, and local recitals, he made his first professional appearance. After seven more years, he made his debut with the Metropolitan Opera. Pavarotti, like Caruso, became the greatest singer of his time because of his parents' leadership. In Luciano's case, his parents stepped aside and let their son make his own decisions.

Expectations and Excellence

I serve as a director of the National Council on Self-Esteem and am deeply involved with the National Council on Youth Leadership. My colleague Jack Canfield, a fellow Self-Esteem Council member and school consultant, has found that two out of three Americans suffer from low self-esteem. He also has found that 80 percent of children entering kindergarten or first grade feel good about themselves.

By the time they reach fifth grade, the number has dropped to 20 percent. And, by the time they become high school seniors, down to 5 percent.

Somewhere along the way, between the ages of six and

sixteen, 75 percent of our kids lose their self-esteem. I consider this to be the greatest waste of natural resources in human history. I would like to see an organization formed to help protect the great inner natural resources of our children. We could even form a national organization.

The immigrants coming into America, especially from the Asian countries, have found enough freedom to become virtually anything in life they set their minds to become. Sanford M. Dornbusch, a professor at Stanford, says that "There is something going on here that we as Americans need to understand." In surveys of seven thousand students in six San Francisco–area high schools, he found that Asian-Americans consistently got better grades than any other group of students. And, this was true regardless of their parents' level of education or their families' social and economic status.

Unfortunately, the longer a young person lives in America, the more acclimated he or she can become to accepting lower standards. This has been demonstrated by a number of studies. A University of Michigan psychologist, Harold W. Stevenson, compared more than seven thousand American grade school students with students in China, Japan, and Taiwan. In mathematics, the Americans performed worse at all grade levels. Stevenson, however, detected no difference in IQ among the groups. This suggests that something significant is happening at home, perhaps even before the children get to school.

The answer is a very simple but powerful leadership difference between Asian and American parents. When Asian parents were asked why their children do well, they most often said, "Because of hard work." American parents, in contrast, credited their kids' success to "talent."

When a child is convinced that he or she has the ability to fulfill high expectations, he or she will very likely live up to those expectations as an adult. To be a real leader with your children, regardless of their ages, teach them that winning is the result of effort, much more than ability. When the report cards and athletic performances are not up to par, encourage them, spend time coaching them, and put more effort into their training.

Ten Do's and Don'ts
of Quality Leadership

Here are ten "do's and don'ts" of leadership that I believe you can apply both in your work and in raising your family. Some of them are my own suggestions and some have been adapted from an excellent book by my friends Dr. William Mitchell and Dr. Charles Paul Conn. The book is *The Power of Positive Parenting*, published by Revell. It's an excellent work for which I had the privilege of writing the foreword.[4]

1. Listen often and as much as possible to what others say, and try to do so without prejudgment.

The act of really listening demonstrates effective leadership as much as any words you might use. If you were fortunate enough to have had a good role model or leader in your life, you can follow his or her example. If you've had to go it alone, and learn from your own mistakes, then try to impart some of that strength to those who are now depending upon you.

2. Don't put anyone off or penalize anyone in any way for asking questions.

If you do, the chances are they'll simply stop asking you and seek answers elsewhere. Or (which would be even worse) they'll go ahead and try to perform a task without sufficient information. As a leader, your primary job is creating winners. Winners depend upon L.U.C.K., which means Laboring Under Correct Knowledge. That correct knowledge must come from *you*.

3. Use praise frequently and sincerely.

There is simply no substitute for enthusiasm on the part of a leader. Try to communicate that what has happened up to now has been good, and that what is going to happen from now on will be even better. The actual words you say matter much less than the timing of when you say them. When Jack Welch became CEO of General Electric in 1981, he installed a direct telephone line to his office for the exclusive use of his purchasing agents. They were instructed to call the moment they had finished negotiating a deal, no matter how small. Welch would always interrupt whatever he was doing to receive the call and congratulate the agent for knocking another dollar or dime off the company's costs. Later, he would send a handwritten letter of thanks.

4. If you feel that criticism is definitely required, don't do it in front of others.

Nothing damages self-esteem as much as being singled out in public. People will be much more receptive to your advice if you offer it quietly, in private. Don't follow the example of Andrew Carnegie, who may have been one of the richest men in American history but who had some serious deficiencies in his "people skills." One day Carnegie was leading some visitors through one of his United States Steel plants when he encountered a weary-looking, elderly employee. "Smith," demanded Carnegie, "how many years have you been working for my company?" "Thirty-nine years," replied the employee, and then he added: "In all those years, I have made only one insignificant mistake." "Very good, Smith," Carnegie muttered, "but in the future, try to be more careful!"

5. Be firm and be fair.

As long as what you're saying is reasonable, people appreciate clearly defined rules, schedules, and boundaries. On the other hand, don't nag or give unnecessary orders. If you do, people will protect themselves by ignoring you.

6. Plan leisure and recreational activities that everyone can do together.

In your work, this can take the form of company outings, retreats, or even something as simple as eating lunch with your subordinates on a regular basis. Many managers also participate in athletic activities with their fellow workers. If you have children, make it a point to take them to your place of business. Show them how you spend your time when you're not with them. Don't separate your family life from your professional life any more than you have to.

7. Don't be afraid to share your concerns with others.

Today, genuine leadership doesn't mean portraying yourself as an invulnerable Great Stone Face—which is, of course, liable to crack at the most inopportune moment. In his book *You Are the Message,* former presidential advisor Roger Ailes describes a situation that occurred when he was working as a television producer. One of the scheduled guests on a talk show was a Marine Corps general who had won the Medal of Honor for his courage in battle. But when Ailes went backstage to talk with him five minutes before air time, the general declared that he was too frightened to go on. Ailes had to think quickly, because he had planned twenty minutes of the program around the war hero. Finally he said, "General, let me put it this way. In just a few minutes you will be introduced, and then you're either going to go out there and talk or I'm going in your place, and I'll tell everybody you're chicken." Ailes describes the general's reaction:

> There was a long pause. He was huge, and I thought he was going to pound me into the floor. But then he smiled. He put his fears into perspective. He contrasted his temporary anxiety with the longer-term confidence he felt about himself. I had kidded him into seeing how absurd it was that a man with the courage to dodge bullets would dodge an

interview. Once he smiled and thought about the funny dissonance of these messages, he was able to relax and return to
his real self. Interestingly, courage isn't the absence of fear.
It is action in the presence of fear. If you feel confident of
yourself as a person, you can admit weakness, even fear and
anxiety, and not imperil your mission.[5]

8. Don't make rash promises and don't be inconsistent.

Broken promises and inconsistency together form a negative
bond of pessimism and a lack of faith in you as a leader.

**9. Whenever you are in a leadership role, focus your
supervision on teaching effective habits and skills, not in
looking for mistakes.**

The best way to foster good habits, of course, is by setting
a good example yourself. Remember: It is much easier to begin
doing things well in the first place, than it is to break bad habits
once they've had a chance to take root. Always make good use
of teachable moments. You can't teach values at prescribed times.
When an event—good or bad—catches the attention of others,
stop and make applications to their lives and beliefs.

**10. Encourage everyone in both your personal and your
professional life to speak up and express their own ideas,
even if you disagree with them.**

Treat them with the same courtesy and respect that you
would like to receive yourself. Moreover, *expect* others to be
successful and *tell* them of your high expectations. People rise to
meet the beliefs of the significant individuals in their lives.

Bringing People Together

Carol Moseley Braun, of Chicago, is a good example of how leadership can and should work in the 1990s.

Although her job as Cook County Recorder of Deeds was hardly a high position on the political totem pole, Carol Braun decided to challenge incumbent Senator Alan Dixon in the Illinois Democratic primary.

In the weeks leading up to the primary, Ms. Braun's poorly financed candidacy was virtually ignored by Senator Dixon. Even political and women's groups that were in agreement with Carol Braun's ideas failed to offer any support, believing that she had no chance for victory. Braun couldn't even afford to run any television ads until the last two weeks of the campaign, when polls showed her trailing far behind Senator Dixon.

But Carol Braun had some important leadership elements working in her favor. Perhaps most important, she recognized the importance of bringing people together, and she was determined to do just that. Growing up on the South Side of Chicago as the daughter of a police officer and a hospital technician, she had joined Martin Luther King, Jr., during the 1960s in demonstrations for equal housing opportunity. With King, she had marched through violently hostile neighborhoods and had seen the destructive effects of pitting one group against another. "We have to connect as people," she often says, "and not allow hatred to divide us."[6]

As it turned out, Carol Braun's unique ability to communicate and to bring people together resulted in a stunning victory in the Illinois primary. In all of American history, there has only been one African-American United States senator, and there has never been an African-American woman in the Senate. By using her talents as a leader, Carol Moseley Braun gave herself a chance to change that.

By the time *The New Dynamics of Winning* is in print, you'll know whether Carol Braun succeeded in getting all the way to Washington. But as I write this, I certainly wouldn't bet against her.

Power from Empowerment

Whether you're a team manager or a corporate leader, I think a good way to think of leadership is as a process of *freeing* your employees to do the best work they can.

A number of years ago, I saw an interview with Pat Riley, who was in the process of winning a string of NBA championships as coach of the Los Angeles Lakers. Riley described his principal coaching task as creating an environment in which his players could *flourish*. In communicating with his team, Riley convinced them that they had the talent to win championships, and that the main goal of the coach was going to be *freeing them* to use that talent. Today Pat Riley is practicing what he preaches in New York.

Today's workers, more than anything else, say they want freedom and autonomy to do their jobs without the boss's interference. As corporate America heads toward the twenty-first century, it's clear that the CEOs of our best-run companies believe that the more power leaders have, the less they should use.

Real power comes by empowering others. Virtually all CEOs polled in a recent *Fortune* magazine survey said they share power much more in the 1990s than they ever did before, and much more than the CEOs before them. Anyone in a leadership position today must realize that power multiplies only when you share it.

The consensus among today's most effective corporate leaders is that the military command-and-control model of leadership went out with smoking, three-martini lunches, and the Berlin Wall. The job of the corporate leader is to set a mission, decide upon a strategic direction, achieve the necessary cooperation, delegate authority—*and then leave people alone.*

Nearly 75 percent of the CEOs surveyed by *Fortune* claim that they have become more participatory and more consensus-oriented. They rely more on communication than on command. No more one-man bands. Today, the emphasis is most definitely on group thinking.

The Five Most Important Words

As I indicated near the beginning of this chapter, listening has become the key skill of the top corporate leader. The CEOs of the best-managed and most profitable companies have cut their staffs and are listening directly to the people who make the products and serve the customers. They are going out in the field and listening directly to the buyer, who is recognized as the true foundation of corporate power.

We need to convert America's companies into championship teams that can hold their own against the rest of the world. To do that, we could take a hint from the late football coach, Paul "Bear" Bryant.

Before his retirement as one of the leading coaches in college football history at Alabama, Bryant observed:

> I'm just a plowhand from Arkansas, but I've learned how to put and hold a team together. I've learned how to lift some individuals up and how to calm others down, until, finally, they've got one heartbeat together, as a team. To do that, there's just three things I'd ever have to say: If anything went wrong, I did it. If it went semi-good, then we did it. If anything went *real* good, then you did it. That's all it takes to get people to win for you.[7]

The key to authentic leadership is to listen to your followers, and then open the door for them to lead themselves. The secret is empowerment. The main incentive is genuine caring and recognition.

The five most important words a leader can speak are: "I am proud of you."

The four most important are: "What is your opinion?"

The three most important are: "If you please."

The two most important are: "Thank you."

And the most important single word of all is: "You"!

Beyond the Arena

A Lifetime Winner

There were ten thousand positive thinkers that day in the arena near Salt Lake City. It was the late 1970s, and I was just reaching my stride as a rally regular. I had just followed Zig Ziglar at the podium, and as I came off the stage, proud of my newly carved niche on the circuit, I paused for a moment and leaned against the wall in back of the arena to catch my breath.

There was an older man standing quietly in the shadows. He was watching the program alone, and at first I didn't recognize him. He nodded at me, smiling, and said, "You're very good. What's your name?"

I told him who I was, and suddenly realized that he was one of my most beloved heroes: John Wooden, the retired head basketball coach at UCLA. The coach with the most wins in the history of college basketball.

"They really loved you and Zig," Coach Wooden said.

"You have a very strong and important message. Stand in the sun while it shines on you and enjoy the warmth. One day, you'll be beyond the arena, in the audience. Savor it now, because success is transient, always in motion, like the game of basketball."

Coach Wooden had been the first speaker of the day, and he'd received a standing ovation as soon as he walked onto the stage. When I walked up on the stage after my introduction, people looked at their programs to see who I was. The audience was saluting him for his forty-year, unparalleled contribution to building winners. They were applauding me for my forty-minute talk.

It's one thing to speak the words, and it's another thing to have devoted your entire life to living them.

In the years since that afternoon, I've reflected many times on my first meeting with John Wooden. From him, I learned never to take myself nor any success I've achieved too seriously. Since then I've maintained contact with Coach Wooden and I've studied his philosophy.

John Wooden exemplifies all the qualities and all the feelings we've discussed in this book. He's been there in the arena and beyond the arena. He believes that real success is *peace of mind.* It comes from the knowledge that you did your best to become the best that you are capable of becoming.

That's really all winning is. Winning is taking the talent and potential you were born with, developing it, and using it fully toward a purpose that makes you feel worthwhile.

Real winners succeed not only in their given specialty or profession, but in their personal lives as well. They set and achieve goals that benefit others as well as themselves. They believe that happiness is not a goal to be chased, but that it's the by-product of living a worthwhile life. Happiness is the natural experience of winning your *own* self-respect, as well as the respect of others.

The Creed of a Champion

When you get to know John Wooden, respect is something that comes naturally. I was in the audience at the San Diego Sports Arena in 1975, when Coach Wooden won his last NCAA title. In all, his UCLA teams won ten national championships in a span of twelve years, and seven in a row. At one point his teams won eighty-eight straight games.

No one's ever come close to that record. Probably, no one ever will.

John Wooden was born in Hall, Indiana, in 1910, one of four sons of a devout couple, living in a modest farmhouse. When he was twelve years old and graduated from the country grade school, his father gave him a seven-point creed, titled "Making the Most of One's Self." He has tried to live his life by it ever since:

1. Be true to yourself.
2. Make each day your masterpiece.
3. Help others.
4. Read good books.
5. Make friendship a fine art.
6. Build a shelter against a rainy day.
7. Pray for guidance, and give thanks for your blessings every day.

Those are simple yet powerful guidelines for living, aren't they? And what a present for a father to give his child upon graduation from grammar school. Ah, but those were the days before Nintendo!

John Wooden became a standout basketball player at Martinsville High and then a star at Purdue University. He is the only person who has made the Hall of Fame both as a player and a coach.

He married his high school sweetheart, Nell, and their life-long love story is one of the most heartwarming I have ever encountered. They were inseparable. They were always a team. Nothing came between their relationship—not scouting trips, not championships, nothing.

Even though Nell died in 1985, Coach Wooden continues to honor her in all his speaking engagements, referring to her as "my sweetheart of sixty years, my wife of fifty-three years, till I lost her." And the greeting cards he sends out still are signed in both their names.

"That pleases Nellie," he says.

Before his career at UCLA, Wooden had taught English at South Bend Central High School and coached at Indiana State for two years. His approach to building champions was that of a teacher. He was certainly unlike the showboating coaches who leap around in front of the TV cameras today.[1]

John Wooden never threw a chair or a tantrum. He didn't yell and scream. Instead, he taught fundamentals, like how to play your own best game, regardless of whom you were playing. He believed his major role was during practice; he viewed the actual game as a final exam that his players took each week. Since he couldn't take it for them or with them, he taught them in practice and then let them play the game and enjoy it.

John Wooden used a simple educational formula. He showed his players the whole game and then broke it down into its basic parts. And he used four basic laws of learning: explanation, demonstration, correction, and repetition. He used a building-block method which he called "The Pyramid of Success." He believes it applies just as much to life beyond the arena as it did to his ten national championship teams. And so do I.

In order to reach the stage of "Competitive Greatness," which was at the top of John Wooden's pyramid, a series of steps had to be taken, each one signifying the mastery of a fundamental trait.

I didn't intend for this book to coincide with John Wooden's general philosophy about building champions, but I'm very pleased to realize that it does. We've tried to look at the whole idea of winning, and then break it down into its basic parts.

First, there's the premise that *mind-set* is what determines the ultimate performance of a champion, not talent or ability. We've explored how winners think and how they train themselves mentally.

Next, we've seen how actual champions from every area of life have applied and lived these principles. Then we've looked at the negative and positive behaviors most common in high-level competition, and learned how you can use corrective feedback to form new, healthy habits.

A Quick Look Back at
The New Dynamics of Winning

Just as aircraft pilots, no matter how experienced, run through a checklist of their plane's systems before taking off, successful people frequently review the techniques that led to their success. So, right now, let's review the major points we've covered in *The New Dynamics of Winning:*

One, *The Drive to Win:*

The key concept in the first chapter is the realization that, early in the game, champions risk playing the fool—because champions know there never was a winner who wasn't at some point a beginner. The greatest risk is the fear of taking action. The greatest security derives from self-determination linked to specific, incremental goals, which becomes a world-class victory like that of Greg LeMond in the Tour de France.

Motivation is a desire for change, and it must be internalized before it has any real power. The fear of change, and even the fear of success, keeps many a person's natural drive for achievement locked in neutral, or in reverse.

How can you motivate yourself toward positive change?

Two, *Paying the Price:*

Commitment is formed at certain vital turning points in your life, when you seize a moment and turn it into an opportunity for altering your destiny.

Remember Mary Lou Retton leaving home in her early teens to train with an outstanding coach? Remember Walter Payton and his off-season runs up the hill? That was their commitment to paying the price of success.

What's yours?

Three, *The Olympian Within:*

This is one of the most critical chapters of all. Think about it, believe it, feel it and share it with those you really care about.

Before the competition even begins, winners *deserve* to win. Performance is only a reflection of internal worth, not a measure of it. What you reveal on the outside is what you feel on the inside. The "inner gold medal" of self-esteem determines the quality of your performance. Before anything else happens, you must believe you are an Olympian within.

Do you believe you *deserve* to win?

Four, *Integrity:*

Before you make any decision, whether it's personal or professional, ask yourself: "Is this true, is this right, is this the honest thing to do?" And don't *tell* your children, your peers, or your subordinates what to do, *show* them.

The material benefits that success brings are wonderful, and the desire to bring them into your life can be a strong motivator. But, to sustain motivation over the long term, there must also be a commitment to human values like honesty, responsibility, and concern for others. Making that commitment, and living up to it every day, is what I mean by integrity.

What does integrity mean to you?

Five, *The Visualization of Victory:*

Visualization works because the mind reacts automatically to the information it receives in the form of feelings, words, and sensory experiences, such as sight, taste, and touch. The mind can't tell the difference between a real experience and one that has been vividly and repeatedly imagined. By mentally rehearsing the perfect accomplishment of your goals, you create a neurological pathway that allows your muscles to repeat those actions. Seeing leads to believing. Believing leads to achieving.

Are you mentally ready to attain your goals?

Six, *Self-Confidence and Self-Transformation:*

Focus all of your attention on what you're doing right now. Trigger words such as: "Easy does it"; "Relax"; "Follow through" are important. Be aware of the silent conversations you have with yourself, and direct them to lead you toward the desired result. "I'm relaxed, ready, focused, and energized. I am calm, confident, and in the zone. *Winning comes naturally to me.*"

Are you clearly focused on the target you've chosen?

Seven, *Strength Through Mental Toughness:*

Remember the Bill Toomey story. Go with the flow, be patient, and don't try to rush success. Think and speak well of your health. Don't make an issue of minor problems or minor ailments. And don't forget the most important element of mental toughness: *Expect the unexpected.* That's what Coach John Wooden's father meant by, "Build a shelter against a rainy day."

Are you hoping for the best, preparing for the worst, and keeping yourself ready for surprises?

Eight, *The "Coachability" Factor:*

The keys to being coachable, to being a team player, are easy to define but not always so easy to act upon. Subordinate your ego needs to the best interests of the group. Be open and inquisitive, but be able to follow instructions. Never assume you have all the answers. Most important of all, be a good listener.

With your family, your friends, and your coworkers, are you a good listener?

Nine, *The Quality of Leadership:*

The foundation of real leadership is empowerment, which is the desire to understand the needs of the people who are depending upon you, and the ability to create an environment in which *they themselves* can fulfill those needs.

As John Welch, CEO of General Electric, said:

If we are going to satisfy customers and win in the marketplace, American managers have got to simplify more, delegate more—and simply *trust more*. We need to drive self-confidence deep into the organization. A company can't distribute self-confidence, but it can foster it by removing layers and giving people a chance to win. We have to undo a 100-year-old concept of leadership and convince our managers that their role is not to control people and stay "on top" of things, but rather to guide, to energize, and to excite.[2]

How can you lead others to do their best?

Life Is Not a Treasure Hunt

Coach John Wooden was an outstanding leader if there ever was one. For many years, he was the greatest and most famous college basketball coach in America. He heard all the cheering crowds, he won all the national championships, he received all the awards.

John Wooden had the greatest triumphs a leader of athletic champions can achieve. And, yet, it was his life beyond the arena that meant the most to him. Without even asking him, I believe he'd give up all those national championships just to hold his wife Nell's hand and be with her again.

That's why something he said to me in the arena that night in Salt Lake City had so much impact. I knew what kind of values Coach Wooden represents. I knew the level of his integrity. I knew the depth of his spiritual faith. Standing in the shadows, he told me that success is a process, not a place you come to.

Coach Wooden quoted Robert Louis Stevenson's wise words, "To travel hopefully is a better thing than to arrive." When you set out to achieve an objective, the hope that is in your heart is more valuable than whatever goals you may attain.

You and I have to understand that *life's most important revelation is that it's the journey that counts, not the destination.* Life is not a treasure hunt. Life itself is the treasure.

Throughout contemporary America—on television, in the movies, in sports, and in business—the message seems to be that life is made up of winners and losers. If you are not number one or in the top five, you've failed. There doesn't seem to be any real reward for simply doing one's best, and enjoying it.

You can spend years reaching one moment of triumph. If you are unhappy through those thousands of minutes leading up to a victory, what good are those few moments of triumph? Life is made up of small pleasures and tiny successes. Family reunions. Intimate moments with a loved one. A baby's first steps. A job

169

well done. Helping a friend. Flying a kite in a good wind. A walk in the country. And even laughing at something stupid you did.

I've always loved rhyme and verse. This is one of my favorites, which I carry in my wallet. It was written by my mother, Irene Waitley. "There isn't more to life, than this: a baby's smile, a loved one's kiss, a book, a tree, a song, a friend, and just a little time to spend."

In conducting the research for this book, I compared my notes on life beyond the arena with some material I had on longevity. I had done a video on the Senior Olympics called *Winning All Our Lives* and I've been working on a book about *Winning in the Glorious Golden Years*.

When I compared the emotional qualities of centenarians, people over a hundred years of age, with those of athletic and business champions, I was amazed at the similarities.

Incredible as it may seem, there are over thirty thousand people in the United States over a hundred years old, and their numbers are increasing rapidly. According to the U.S. Census Bureau, this is the fastest-growing age group in the nation's population.

I knew that George Burns had booked the London Palladium for his one hundredth birthday party, but I never realized that, by that time, he could fill the New Orleans Superdome with seventy thousand of his hundred-year-old fans, cheering him by satellite, and doing the wave!

By the time I reach one hundred years of age, in the year 2033, I expect to get a fax from the third female president of the United States, congratulating me along with the other one million Americans who also will celebrate their hundredth birthday the same year. That's incredible, isn't it! There will be a million Americans over one hundred years of age in roughly forty years.

So what do these super-senior champions and other winners have in common?

A Passion for Living

Discounting genetic factors, one of the most important keys to living a long life is, quite simply, to have a passion for living. This excitement about being alive is one of the most attractive qualities you can possess. In fact, if you want a teammate or lifemate to love to be around you, all you need to do is love to be around.

No one has a greater passion for life than I do, and here's one reason why:

In 1979, I was booked on a flight from Chicago to Los Angeles. I was on my way to a speaking engagement before going home for the weekend. I had to run for the plane, and became very upset when I saw the gate agent lock the door and then saw the mobile ramp pull away from the plane. I argued and begged and told her I had to be on that nonstop DC-10, Flight 191 to L.A., or I would miss my speech.

The plane taxied away from the ramp and out toward the runway despite my protests. I stormed out of the boarding area and back to the ticket counter to register my complaint.

Standing in line at the counter, about twenty minutes later, I heard the news that the plane had crashed on takeoff with no survivors. An engine had broken loose and fallen back onto the runway. The hydraulic lines and control cables had been severed and there was nothing the pilots could do to control the aircraft.

I left the ticket line, booked a room at the airport hotel, kneelt down beside my bed in prayer, and tried to get some sleep.

It's been over a decade since then, but I still have my unvalidated ticket for Flight 191. I never turned it in to my travel agent for a refund. Instead, I tacked it on a bulletin board in my office at home as a silent reminder.

About once a year I get a little annoyed with some injustice in the world that has made me a victim of the system and I grouse around the house. My wife, Susan, gently takes me by the hand to my bulletin board for a look at my still-unused ticket on Flight 191. And, I realize, once again, that every day is Christmas for me. Just being alive is a fabulous gift!

When my eyes open each morning, I look at my wife, smile, and say, I love you. I also think to myself: Wonderful, safe again, another new day. Let's go!

The Most Marvelous Game of All

Another bond that centenarians and other champions share is a *real love for their life's work.*

In fact, they don't consider their careers to be work. It's like Willie Stargell, the retired baseball star, once remarked that at the start of a ballgame, you never hear an umpire yelling, "Work ball." Of course not. They always yell, "Play Ball!"

And that's what life is, or ought to be—a marvelous game.

You might question the comparison between your own life and that of a professional athlete. But stop to consider how many commercial fishermen would rather be gardening, or how many professional gardeners would rather be fishing. Even many athletes consider the season a grind. The majority of people think of their work merely as a means to an end.

The challenge, therefore, is to be totally committed every day to pursuing your life's purpose as you have defined it. That's certainly what John Wooden is doing. Today, he's in his eighth decade, yet you'll see John Wooden staging summer basketball camps for young people. You probably won't meet famous NBA players there, but you probably will learn the game of basketball, and a great deal about the game of life.

The True Arena of Champions

One former pro-basketball player's life has taken a tragic turn outside the arena, yet in my view this has enhanced his stature as a champion far beyond any three-point shots or pressure-packed free throws.

Earvin Johnson grew up in East Lansing, Michigan. He came from a loving family, but there wasn't much money. His family couldn't afford to buy him a bike, so young Earvin walked everywhere. And everywhere he walked, he dribbled a basketball, and learned to do "magic" things with it.

As a college sophomore, he led Michigan State to the NCAA championship. Then on to the Los Angeles Lakers: Five NBA championships, and three awards as the league's Most Valuable Player.

Johnson never led the league in scoring, yet he probably could have if he'd wanted to. But he always preferred making a great pass to scoring a basket. He made everyone around him a better player. His teammates knew that if they were open, Magic would get them the ball. He was like a coach on the court. He almost always made the right play, because he thought of the team's needs rather than his own. He may have been the most unselfish superstar ever to play the game. If you asked him if that unselfishness had hurt his income or his career, Magic would simply break into his famous smile and say: "I just love playing basketball." And he meant it.

With the discovery of his infection by HIV—Human Immunodeficiency Virus—Magic Johnson retired from professional basketball, but he certainly didn't stop being a hero. On the contrary, he became a greater hero than ever through the courage he displayed in confronting his infection, his efforts to bring the problems of people with AIDS to public and governmental awareness, and his work with young people to provide further information about the disease.

For Magic Johnson, another, truer championship arena lay beyond the boundaries of the basketball court. That arena exists wherever a human being faces a challenge and fights bravely to overcome it, not just for himself or herself, but for the benefit of everyone.

I urge you to enter that championship arena.

Life is never just being. It is *becoming* and *creating*.

Don't waste your time accumulating objects or attributes that will mean nothing to you after a few years. Real value comes from whatever you create in beauty and goodness and truth.

Inspired by the words of Alexander Schindler, when you create love in a house, you will have a home.

When you add pride to a city, you have a community.

Bring learning to a pile of bricks, and you have a school.

Find religion in the most modest structure, and you have a sanctuary.

Foster justice in all human endeavor, and you have a civilization.

Put them all together, add your own hopes and your own unique gifts, and you have a future lit with the radiant flame of the Olympic torch. Pass this torch along to everyone you meet. In it burns the soul and spirit of a champion.

The Twenty-one-Day Plan

The final section of *The New Dynamics of Winning* is a twenty-one-day training program to prepare you for your own personal Olympiad: the "competition" which includes literally everything you do every day throughout your personal and professional life. Unlike the athletes you've read about in the preceding pages, your challenge is not to run faster, jump higher, or score more points in a basketball game. Instead, you want to learn the *process* of winning, by developing all the resources of your mind and body to the fullest.

During the twenty-one days, the Plan asks you to set and achieve two goals, one personal and one career-related. But over and above these specific objectives, the Plan provides a method for looking at your life in an organized and highly motivated way. Regardless of the results you achieve in attaining particular goals, the Plan will be successful if it inspires you to continue to put your objectives in writing, to break them down into manageable subgoals, and to use *The New Dynamics of Winning* to attain them.

To gain maximum benefit from the Plan, try to think of this section as a sort of personal trainer in print. Occasionally, one day's training may refer back to a previous day's, so it's important to follow the sequence from beginning to end.

The only supplies you'll need are a little time, a small notebook, and a pen or pencil. And remember: You are an athlete in training!

Day One: Monday

Winning begins with feeling good about yourself, referring to yourself in positive terms, and seeing yourself as a winner. That doesn't mean you'll turn into an arrogant or overbearing person. On the contrary, the ability to see yourself in a positive light will make everyone around you feel better about themselves as well.

- On the first pages of your notebook, write a "résumé" listing all your skills, talents, and unique abilities. Be sure to consider both your personal and your professional qualities.

- Look over your résumé and ask yourself the following question: *Which of your personal and professional abilities have the greatest practical potential for development in the next twenty-one days?*

- Now, based on the individual assessment you've just made, write down *one personal and one professional goal that you will achieve by Day Nineteen of this twenty-one-day program.*

Why Day Nineteen? Because Day Twenty is kept in reserve for contingency planning. And Day Twenty-One is your reward day!

Day Two: Tuesday

Begin the day by reading over the résumé you wrote yesterday. Do this often from now on. The list you've made of your best qualities can be a valuable resource for affirmations, visualizations, and positive self-talk.

Now look back at the two goals you've set for completion during the course of the Plan. In your notebook, write down the answers to these questions:

- What *physical resources* will you need in order to achieve these goals?

- What *additional knowledge* will you require?

- What *behavior patterns* will you need to change?

- Today, and every day from now on, ask yourself this question whenever you're faced with a decision: ''Which alternative brings me closest to achieving my ultimate objectives?'' Then act accordingly.

Tomorrow you'll begin taking well-planned, practical action toward realizing your goals.

Day Three:
Wednesday

An incremental, stair-step approach is by far the best way to ensure success. To put this technique to work, refer again to the personal and professional goals you wrote on Day One. Then, for each goal, create *two intermediate subgoals* as follows:

- Make the first pair of subgoals things you can do *today*—and then make sure you do them! In addition to the practical benefits, actually taking steps toward your personal and professional objectives will have important benefits for your self-esteem. These immediate subgoals don't have to be major advances. Just ask yourself what you can do in the next twenty-four hours that will bring you closer to your goals.

- For your second pair of subgoals, set a target date for completion of *one week from today*. That will leave you with ten days for final achievement of your objectives. To be most effective, your subgoals should present a challenge, but they shouldn't be strenuous. They should be out of your immediate reach—but not out of sight.

Now, close your notebook. It's time to go out and take immediate action toward your goals.

Day Four: Thursday

Did you successfully achieve the immediate and professional sub-goals you set yesterday? If not, carry them over to today.

As a winner, you naturally express everything in positive terms. Even problems and setbacks can be looked at optimistically.

- In your notebook, write down one- or two-sentence descriptions of some of your most pressing problems. Then, imagine that these were not your problems, but those of a trusted friend who had come to you for advice. How would you provide encouragement for your friend by pointing out the *opportunities* hidden within the apparent difficulty? Write it down!

- List three necessary but possibly unpleasant tasks that you've been putting off. Decide exactly what you need to do in order to get these tasks over with once and for all, and estimate how much time will be required. Finally, set a specific target date for completion—one that falls before the end of the Plan.

Day Five: Friday

Learn to wake up feeling happy and optimistic about the coming day. For example, it's helpful to awaken to music rather than an alarm, a commercial, or depressing morning news reports.

- What other changes can you make so that each day gets off to a positive start? Do you eat a healthy breakfast? Do you dress to look your best? Do you allow yourself enough time to get ready for the day?

- Throughout the day, what rewards can you build into your schedule to sustain your positive outlook? What negative influences should you be sure to avoid?

- Make a real effort all day to smile at everyone you meet and to refer to others in positive terms. At the end of the day, think back on the specific occasions when you did these things. How did others respond? How did you respond when people approached you cheerfully and helpfully?

Day Six: Saturday

Don't forget: next Wednesday is the target date for your second pair of personal and professional subgoals!

Once again, read the positive résumé on the first pages of your notebook. Think of all the good things, no matter how big or small, that have happened to you *since* you wrote the résumé. Now write down brief descriptions of your new positive experiences.

- Today, set aside fifteen minutes to visualize the specific achievements you're currently striving for. As you imagine your success, be sure to experience the satisfaction you'll feel when your goals are actually attained.

- During the past week, have you shared your goals with others? It's important to avoid doing so with negative people or cynics. Share your goals only with people who really care about you and want to help.

- Right now, think of a specific individual who can provide help, inspiration, or support for your plans. Make it a point to contact that person today, or on Monday at the latest.

Day Seven: Sunday

Sunday, of course, is traditionally a day for reflection. Here are some questions that can help you see yourself in a new perspective. Write your responses in your notebook.

- Try to imagine how others see you. Write a description of yourself from the point of view of your boss, your coworkers, or your friends and family.

- Complete a paragraph that begins, "When people meet me for the first time, they think . . ."

- Now write another paragraph that begins, "When people meet me for the first time, *I would like them to think . . .*"

- What specific things can you do in the coming week that will shrink the discrepancy between the two paragraphs you've just written?

Day Eight: Monday

One quality shared by winners in all areas of life is the ability to remain mentally and physically relaxed under pressure. In most cases, however, this is not a quality they were born with. "Keeping cool" is a *skill* they learned, and you can learn it, too.

- Make a list of the people and situations that cause you to feel anxious and pressured. What can you do differently from now on to reduce their influence?

- If you don't have a regular exercise routine, plan one right now. Healthy exercise is one of the best methods of defusing stress. What are some other things you can do on a regular basis that will help you relax?

- Whenever you feel pressured, run a "mental video" of positive images. Visualize all the times you've faced challenges in the past and come out on top. Even if you're severely pressed for time, don't be afraid to take a minute or so to watch this personal-highlight film. You'll return to your task with renewed optimism and confidence.

Day Nine: Tuesday

Tomorrow is the date you set for your second personal and professional subgoals!

The self-image that you show to the world is the external manifestation of your internal sense of self-esteem. Here are some topics that will help you clarify your self-image and discover opportunities for improvement.

- Are you happy with the way you dress? If not, set aside some money to buy some clothes that will make you feel good about yourself. And if you have any clothes in your closet that you haven't worn in the past year, get rid of them *now*!

- If there's clutter in your car, desk, garage, dresser drawers, or anywhere else, make cleaning it up an important priority, even if no one sees it except you. *Especially* if no one sees it except you!

- Do other people compliment you on your appearance? What specific adjustments can you make so that you'll stand out in a positive way among your peers? Think of something you can do *today*!

Day Ten:
Wednesday

By today's end, you will have achieved the final subgoals for the personal and professional objectives you set at the beginning of the Plan. The next step is to accomplish the goals themselves!

- Once you've attained your subgoals, how can you structure your time over the next ten days to approach your final goals confidently and without stress?

- Think of two *new* people who can help you achieve your goals. Make it a point to contact them today.

- Whenever you think of your goals, silently repeat to yourself: "I want to—I can—I will!" Before long, you'll do this automatically.

One note of caution: Sometimes the drive to achieve can lead you to take on more than you should. If your experience during the past week leads you to believe that your goals need adjustment, don't be afraid to do so. Life is a marathon, not a sprint. Learning to pace yourself is an important part of being a winner.

Day Eleven:
Thursday

On Day Four of the Plan, you were asked to list three necessary tasks that you had been putting off, and to set a date for their completion. Now is a good time to see where you stand. If you haven't completed these tasks, make a commitment to do so before a specific date.

If you've been experiencing difficulty, *procrastination* is probably to blame. Answering the questions below can help you overcome your inertia.

- How can you make yourself aware of procrastination? What are some of the things you tell yourself when you're trying to put something off?

- Deadlines are an important component of time management, but they can be intimidating and counterproductive if they're not formulated carefully. How can you create *positive* deadlines for the tasks you've been postponing? How can you reward yourself for meeting the deadlines?

- If you're like many procrastinators, you may be unconsciously enlisting the aid of others to help you waste time. If that's the case, how can you break this pattern? How can other people help you overcome a procrastination habit?

Day Twelve: Friday

It's natural to compare yourself with others, but as you do so, there are things to watch out for. Winners know they don't really compete against others. Success means doing your best according to the standards you set for yourself.

- Winners, paradoxically, accept themselves exactly as they are now, but they're also making constant changes. What self-improvement, however small, can you put into effect today?

- Can you think of another person you would rather be? If so, write out a description of how you imagine that person's life. Do you still prefer his or her life to your own? What can you do to close the gap?

- Think of three people who are doing exactly what you would *like* to be doing. Make a plan for getting in touch with these people in order to benefit from their experiences. If they're genuine winners, they'll probably be happy to share what they've learned.

Day Thirteen:
Saturday

The term *comfort zones* refers to patterns of thought and behavior that have become almost like reflexes. In your comfort zones, your actions are no longer a matter of choice. Instead, you're just doing things because that's the way you've always done them.

Saturday is a good day for testing the environment outside your comfort zones. Here are some suggestions:

- Unplug your TV for the day. Better yet, put it in the closet. Incredible as the idea may seem, you might find that the closet is just the right place for it!

- Visit your local library. If you don't already have a card, they'll issue you a temporary one on the spot when you show proper identification. Then take out three books at random, *without looking at the titles*. Take them home and, no matter what they turn out to be, make a real effort to read them.

- Set your alarm for thirty minutes earlier than usual, and leave it there for at least a week. Now you've got an extra half-hour of living outside your comfort zone. Make the most of it!

Day Fourteen:
Sunday

In Chapter Two of *The New Dynamics of Winning,* you read how baseball great Mike Schmidt encountered his "moment of truth" when he was almost killed in an accident at the age of five. As you'll recall, a moment of truth can be any event, good or bad, that becomes a turning point in your life. It's when you make a commitment to point your life in a specific direction.

- What was your moment of truth? As you look back on your life, what was the turning point? In your notebook, describe this event and what it means to you.

- Note: Perhaps you've had more than one moment of truth—or maybe you can't identify a particular point when you decided to take control of your own destiny. If that's the case, *then how about right now?*

Day Fifteen:
Monday

Today is the beginning of the Plan's final week. By now you've made real progress toward the personal and professional goals you've chosen.

As we discussed on Day Eight, always include *visualization* as an integral part of your daily schedule. Here's a quick review of the four-step visualization process:

- Imagine dynamic scenes filled with action and movement.

- Picture both the successful achievement of your goal and the steps leading up to it.

- Visualize only conditions and events that are in your best interest and the best interests of all concerned.

- Most important, always visualize in the "present tense." Experience the satisfaction of doing what you set out to do, as if you're achieving your goal *right now*!

You should also develop a short, affirmative, present-tense statement that describes the performance you intend to achieve. Whenever you visualize, use this statement as an affirmation to accompany the successful completion of your task.

Day Sixteen: Tuesday

On Day Six, we suggested that you think of a specific person to help you achieve your goals, either through practical assistance or by providing inspiration and support. Have you succeeded in getting in touch with the individual you chose?

If you haven't been able to make contact, try dropping a note, or perhaps an overnight-express letter, to the person you chose. If you still don't get a response, reach out to someone new.

- What kinds of people should you be associating with in order to achieve your goals as soon as possible? Make a list of five personal characteristics you should look for.

- If someone were to come to *you* for help in attaining success, would you be willing? What possible benefits could there be for you?

Day Seventeen: Wednesday

Remember decathlon champion Bill Toomey's guidelines for contingency planning: "Expect the best, plan for the worst, and be prepared for a surprise!" Here are some suggestions for applying these principles in your life. Write your responses in your notebook:

- Are you expecting something really good to happen today? What can you do right now to make your expectation come true?

- If everything you've planned for today turns out badly, will you be able to accept it and still look forward to tomorrow? How can you mentally prepare yourself so that you're able to do this?

- In spite of your most careful preparations, when have you been *surprised* by the way things turned out? What did you learn about being able to adjust to unexpected developments? Think of three specific instances.

Day Eighteen: Thursday

Tomorrow is the date you targeted for achieving your specified personal and professional goals!

True leadership is not about power, but about empowerment. As Pat Riley expressed it when he was coaching the Los Angeles Lakers, his task as a leader was to provide an environment in which his players could *flourish*.

- In your work and in your personal life, who are the people who are looking to you for leadership? How can you help them flourish?

- Who are you depending upon for leadership? Is he or she giving you a sense of empowerment? If not, what can you do to make your needs clear?

- Are you being a good leader to yourself? Do you encourage yourself to take risks, and to focus on the probability of success rather than the possibility of failure?

Day Nineteen: Friday

Congratulations! By today's end, you'll have achieved both the personal and the professional goals you set for yourself at the beginning of this Plan. One of the best reasons for setting deadlines is the sense of accomplishment you experience when you meet or beat them. You deserve a reward!

- Buy yourself something you want but don't really need. If you can't quite afford it, buy it anyway. Don't worry about going overboard. You've shown yourself to be a highly responsible person, and you've earned the right to splurge a little.

- Then get a present of equal value for someone you care about. It should come as a complete surprise. Rewarding yourself is more fun when you include someone else, and maybe he or she will do the same for you someday soon.

If in fact you haven't achieved your goals yet, make Saturday your "catch up day." Try not to put anything on your agenda for tomorrow except doing everything possible to attain the objectives you set for yourself.

Day Twenty:
Saturday

The purpose of The Twenty-One-Day Plan was to show you the mechanics and the benefits of setting objectives, monitoring your progress, and achieving your goals. If you've accomplished what you set out to do, that's great, and you should be proud of yourself. If you haven't yet, use today to catch up. And even if you don't meet your goals, *you are a winner* as long as you've done your best. Keep trying, and nothing can stand in your way. Remember:

- Life is a treasure, not a treasure hunt.

- Success is a journey, not a destination.

- "To travel hopefully is a better thing than to arrive."

Day Twenty-one: Sunday

Today, reward yourself for what you've *tried* to accomplish, and for what you *have* accomplished, and *for just being you*!

> Not in Utopia—subterranean fields—
> Or some secreted island, Heaven knows where!
> But in this very world, which is the world
> Of all of us—the place where, in the end,
> We find our happiness, or not at all!
>   —William Wordsworth

N O T E S

CHAPTER ONE

1. Thomas J. Watson, Jr., *Father, Son & Co.* (New York: Bantam Books, 1990), p. 291.
2. Donald E. Petersen, *A Better Idea* (Boston: Houghton Mifflin, 1991), p. 6.

CHAPTER TWO

1. *The Wall Street Journal,* February 7, 1992.
2. *Current Biography Yearbook,* 1986, p. 462.
3. Peter Hay, *The Book of Business Anecdotes* (New York: Facts on File), p. 213.
4. Ibid., p. 188.
5. Ibid., p. 109.
6. Ibid., p. 103.
7. *Parade Magazine,* July 15, 1990, p. 10.
8. Doris Lee McCoy, *Megatraits* (Plano, Texas: Wordware, 1988), pp. 208–209.
9. *The Wall Street Journal,* February 7, 1992.

CHAPTER THREE

1. *The New York Times,* February 11, 1992.
2. Terry Orlick, *In Pursuit of Excellence* (Champaign, Illinois: Leisure, 1990), p. 34.
3. Bruce Ogilvie, Address to National Figure Skating Coaches, Vail, Colorado, May 1990.
4. Ibid.

5. *The Book of Business Anecdotes*, p. 109.
6. Ibid., p. 274.
7. Ted W. Engstrom, *The Pursuit of Excellence* (Zondervan, 1982).
8. Terry Orlick, *In Pursuit of Excellence* (Champaign, Illinois: Leisure, 1990), p. 38.

CHAPTER FOUR
1. *Inc.* magazine, February 1992, p. 66.
2. *Newsweek,* March 2, 1992.
3. John Hillkirk and Gary Jacobson, *Grit, Guts and Genius: True Tales of Mega-Success* (Boston: Houghton Mifflin, 1991), p. 99.
4. Doron P. Levin, *Irreconcilable Differences: Ross Perot versus General Motors* (Boston: Little, Brown, 1989), p. 194.
5. *Washington Post Magazine,* April 12, 1987, p. 73.
6. *The Book of Business Anecdotes,* p. 147.
7. *Bits and Pieces* (New Jersey: Economic Press, April 1987), p. 2.
8. Alexander Hiam, *The Vest-Pocket CEO* (Englewood Cliffs, New Jersey: Prentice Hall), pp. 57–58, quoting Maseo Nemoto, *Total Quality Control for Management,* trans. David Lu.
9. *The New York Times,* April 6, 1992.

CHAPTER FIVE
1. Richard M. Restak, M.D., *The Mind* (New York: Bantam, 1988), p. 16.
2. *The Vest-Pocket CEO*, pp. 68–70, citing Michael Ray and Rochelle Myers, *Creativity in Business* (Doubleday).
3. Mike Samuels and Nancy Samuels, *Seeing with the Mind's Eye* (New York: Random House, 1975), pp. 223–225.
4. Stephen King, interview with W. C. Stroby, *Writer's Digest,* March 1992, p. 22.

CHAPTER SIX
1. *The Book of Business Anecdotes,* p. 109.

CHAPTER SEVEN
1. Warren Bennis, *On Becoming a Leader* (New York: Addison Wesley, 1990), p. 58.

2. *Grit, Guts, and Genius: True Tales of Mega-Success,* pp. 199–210.

CHAPTER EIGHT

1. *The Book of Business Anecdotes,* p. 269.
2. Sara Noble, ed., *301 Great Management Ideas from America's Most Innovative Small Companies* (Boston: *Inc.* Publishing, 1991), p. 56.
3. Orel Hershiser with Jerry B. Jenkins, *Out of the Blue* (Brentwood, Tennessee: Wolgemuth & Hyatt, 1989), pp. 9–13.

CHAPTER NINE

1. *Tao-te Ching,* trans. Stephen Mitchell (New York: Harper & Row, 1989), p. 100.
2. Ted Engstrom, *The Best of Ted Engstrom* (San Bernadino, California: Here's Life Publishers, 1988), p. 81.
3. Luciano Pavarotti, *Choose One Chair* (Guideposts, March 1985), p. 40.
4. William Mitchell and C. P. Conn, *The Power of Positive Parenting* (Old Tappon, New Jersey: Fleming H. Revell, 1989), pp. 34–35.
5. Roger Ailes, *You Are the Message* (Doubleday, 1989), pp. 160–162.
6. *The Wall Street Journal,* March 20, 1992.
7. *Bits and Pieces,* October 1983, p. 24.

CHAPTER TEN

1. Alexander Wolff, *The Coach and His Champion, Sports Illustrated,* 1989, pp. 59–70.
2. *Fortune,* March 26, 1990.

DISCOVER THE POWER
OF AUDIO LEARNING WITH
NIGHTINGALE-CONANT

You can learn new skills for success, high-power motivation, and strategies for self-improvement and goal setting.

And you can learn ANYTIME or ANYWHERE! Wherever you can listen to audiocassettes—in your car, on a walk, working around the house, on a plane or a train.

As the world's leading publisher of self-development audio programs, **Nightingale-Conant** is a unique learning resource. In our full-color, 64-page catalog you can find audiocassette programs that teach you how to improve all areas of your life.

If you enjoyed this book, then you'll want to hear Denis Waitley speaking on this and other important topics. His audio programs available from Nightingale-Conant include:

✔ **The New Dynamics of Winning** (audio version)   6 cassettes   708A
   Gain the mind-set of a champion
✔ **The Psychology of Winning**   6 cassettes   7161A
   A million-copy best-seller
✔ **Seeds of Greatness**   6 cassettes   7001A
   The ten best-kept secrets of total success

✔ **How to Build Your Child's Self-Esteem**   6 cassettes   699A
  Help children become strong and self-assured

✔ **The Psychology of Human Motivation**   8 cassettes   609A
  The latest on what motivates top achievers

To order programs or request a free catalog *call* **1-800-525-9000.**
Use the coupon on the book jacket to receive $20 off on your order!

Nightingale-Conant

NIGHTINGALE-CONANT CORPORATION
7300 North Lehigh Avenue • Niles, Illinois 60714
1-708-647-0300 • 1-800-323-5552